Failure of Small Businesses

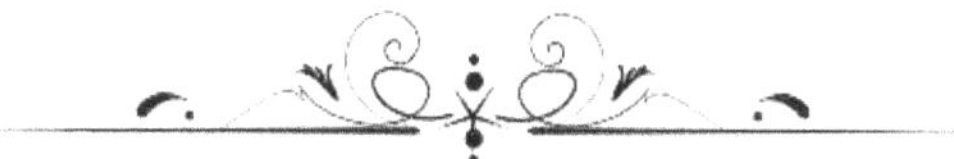

"I was shocked to find that limited funding was the major cause of failure of small businesses against my expectation that lack of leadership played a major role in causing the phenomenon."

Dr. Evans Nyatigo Ongaga

FAILURE OF SMALL BUSINESSES IN SAN JOSE, CALIFORNIA: A PHENOMENOLOGICAL STUDY

BY

DR. EVANS NYATIGO ONGAGA

STUDY SUPERVISION

NANCY WOOD, PHD

ALICIA HOLLAND, EDD

SANDRA D. NUNN, DM

School of Advanced Studies
University of Phoenix

American Journal *of*
Transformational Leadership

ProQuest Dissertations
ProQuest Databases

Texas International
Guardian, Inc.

Cover design and book design *by Dr. Anthony Obi Ogbo,*
Production *by International Guardian*
Publishing: *American Journal of Transformational Leadership*

This book is a reproduction of studies based on a Dissertation presented by
Evans Nyatigo Ongaga in partial fulfillment of the requirements for the degree
Doctor of Management in Organizational Leadership
Research Study Supervision
Nancy Wood, PhD
Alicia Holland, EdD
Sandra D. Nunn, DM

Research Study Approval
William C. Beck II, PhD
Academic Dean, School of Advanced Studies,
University of Phoenix

DEDICATION

The dissertation is dedicated to my beloved father, the late Stanley Ongaga. Before passing on in 1998 as a retired high school teacher and principal, my father inspired and encouraged me to pursue education to the highest level. Here I am feeling his spirits and presence and delighted for the dream come true as I complete the academic journey.

The dissertation is also dedicated to my mother who is going stronger at her senior age. Though far away in Africa, my mother's Christian way of life and unconditional love motivates me in my daily endeavors. Furthermore, I dedicate the document to my beloved son Arnold and wish him a quick recovery. I pray to Almighty to alleviate the pain he is undergoing to start leading normal life again.

APPRECIATION

In a special way, I would like to recognize the Committee Members: Dr. Alicia Holland, and Dr. Sandra G. Nunn who replaced Dr. Karen Bammel. Dr. Sandra G. Nunn accepted to join aboard and offered the necessary support when most needed. The members stayed involved until the end of the dissertation. Many thanks go to the Chair, Dr. Nancy Wood for an outstanding direction and leadership in the entire project duration. I express my gratitude to everyone for the inspiring and encouraging me particularly in the intense moments of the project. Special acknowledgment also goes to small business owner-leaders who volunteered willingly to share the lived experiences concerning the failure of the small businesses. The participation of the small business owner-leaders resulted in the success of the study. Lastly, I would like to recognize my son, Arnold for persevering with his sick condition as I spent more time in the worthwhile bruising academic journey. We both have strong faith in God's power.

ABSTRACT

A qualitative phenomenological intrinsic study was used to explore the lived experiences of 10 Small Business owner-leaders who experienced failure of small businesses in San Jose, California. Varied factors contributing to the failure of small businesses include poor leadership, limited resources and funding difficulties, poor location and planning. Small business owner-leaders who participated in the interviews were asked to describe lived experiences to enhance the phenomenon's understanding. Modified van Kaam approach was applied to comprehend the participants' lived experiences concerning the phenomenon of failure of small businesses. The emerging and developing nine themes replicated the participants' perceptions that an interplay of many factors, lack of resources and limited funding including bad credit and lack of collateral securities, lack of knowledge and understanding, poor leadership involving not people-oriented, poor business operations, closed most days, lack of trust, communication and customer service, economic crisis including underdevelopment of the economy, poor business location, such as, un-strategic and low populated areas,

ABSTRACT

lack of motivation and inspiration, culture - some goods are slowly consumed based on the culture of the people in the community, size - expansion of small businesses results in funding difficulties, and poor planning results in lack of business understanding and knowledge, and improper business assessment that results in failure of small businesses. Owner-leaders of small businesses consistently identified and described lack of resources as the primary cause of small business failure, which was attributed to underperformance in leadership.

TABLE OF CONTENTS

X List of Tables

X List of Figures

I ▪ **Chapter I: Introduction**

1 Introduction

3 Background of the Problem

9 Problem Statement

12 Purpose of the Study

13 Significance of the Study

17 Nature of Study

19 Research Questions

21 Theoretical Framework

22 Definition of Terms

24 Assumptions

25 Scope

25 Limitations

26 Delimitation

27 Summary

II ▪ **Chapter 2: Review of the Literature**

31 Title Searches, Articles, Research Documents, Journals

32 Historical Perspective

33 Impact of Small Businesses 2

35 Failure Rates and Small Businesses

36 Common Definitions of Failure

38 Analysis of Failure Definitions and Literature

40 Failure Defined and Context of Study

41 Small Business Failure and Understanding of Causes

51 Small Business Failure and Research Methodologies

57 Gaps in Literature Review

59 Conclusion

60 Summary

III ▪ **Chapter 3: Research Methods**

65 Research Method and Appropriateness

68 Research Design and Appropriateness

75 Research and Sub-Research Questions

78 Interviews

80 Population, Sampling Frame, Data Collection

84 Confidentiality

85 Informed Consent

86 Geographic Location

87 Instrumentation

90 Gathering of Personal Experiences

91 Reliability and Validity

95 Analysis of Personal Experiences

96 Summary

IV ▪ **Chapter 4: Results**

101 Discussion of Research Methodology

101 Research Sampling Procedures

104 Sample Selection and Descriptions

105 Demographics and Biological Data

107 Pilot Study

109 Interview Process

111 The process of Data Analysis

118   Findings

119   Reduction and Elimination

159   Summary

V ▪ **Chapter 5: Conclusions and Recommendations**

162   Review of the Study

165   Implications of the Study and Finding

184   Recommendations

191   Limitations and Future Research

193   Summary

197   References

---

223   *Appendix A*: Interview Questions

225   *Appendix B:* Informed Consent

227   *Appendix C:* Letter Requesting Participation

229   *Appendix D:* Letter of Appreciation to Participate

231   *Appendix E:* Word Frequency Query - Summary

235   *Appendix F:* Reductions and Eliminations
                Interview Questions 10 - 15

237   About the Author

LIST OF TABLES

105 *Table 1: Demographic Features (Participants) Gender*

106 *Table 2: Demographic Features (Participants) Age*

116 *Table 3: Horizonalization: Relevant Expressions*

122 *Table 4: Lack of Funding and Limited resources*

123 *Table 5: Poor Leadership*

123 *Table 6: Lack of Knowledge and Skills*

124 *Table 7: Poor Customer Service*

125 *Table 8: Government Policy and Regulations*

125 *Table 9: Lack of Resources and Limited Funding*

126 *Table 10: Lack of Knowledge*

127 *Table 11: Lack of Advertisement*

128 *Table 12: Lack of Resources and Limited Funding*

129 *Table 13: Lack of Knowledge*

130 *Table 14: Unfavorable Competition*

130 *Table 15: Poor Location*

131 *Table 16: Lack of Resources and Limited Funding*

132 *Table 17: Lack of Knowledge*

132 *Table 18: High Operating Costs……... 115*

133 *Table 19: Lack of Knowledge, Education and Training*

134 *Table 20: Lack of Leadership and Poor Operations*

135 *Table 21: Lack of Knowledge and Education*

137 *Table 22: Lack of Knowledge, Education and Poor Resource*

138 *Table 23: Lack of Leadership*

139 *Table 24: Misallocation of Resources   121*

140 *Table 25: Lack of Resources and Funding Difficulties*

141 *Table 26: Economic Underdevelopment*

142 *Table 27: Unemployment*

142 *Table 28: Low Tax Revenue*

143 *Table 29: Poor Leadership*

145 *Table 30: Lack of Motivation and Inspiration*

146   *Table 31: Inability to Motivate and Inspire*

147   *Table 32: Lack of Motivation and Inspiration*

148   *Table 33: Poor Location*

150   *Table 34: Culture*

151   *Table 35: Lack of Resources and Funding Difficulties*

153   *Table 36: Poor Planning*

154   *Table 37: Size.*

155   *Table 38: Limited Resources ....*

LIST OF FIGURES

105   *Figure 1: Chart – Demographic Features (Participants) Gender*

106   *Figure 2: Chart – Demographic Features (Participants) Age*

110   *Figure 3: Visual Presentation of the Interview Process*

115   *Figure 4: Steps Used for Analyzing the Data*

117   *Figure 5: Word Frequency Query - Word cloud*

118   *Figure 6: Word Frequency Query - Tree Map*

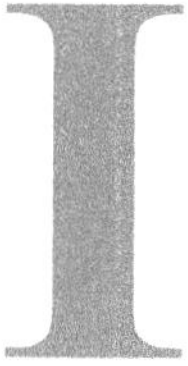

Chapter 1
Introduction

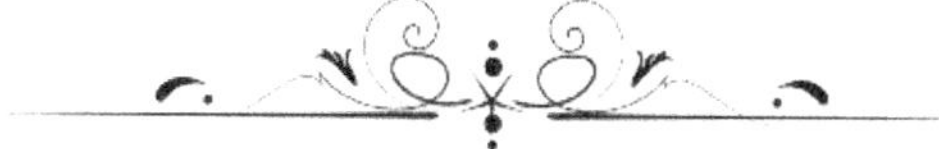

■ The key intellectual curiosity for the current study was to understand the inability of small businesses to maintain low failure rates.

The number of small businesses operating in the United States is 23 million (Cronin-Gilmore, 2012, p. 96; Heady, Maples, & Greco, 2005, p. DE41; Kobe, 2007a, p. 1). Small business sales account for 54% of all U.S. total sales (U.S. Census Bureau, 2014). Researchers of the existing studies indicated the invaluable role of small businesses in enhancing the prosperity of the U.S. economy by creating job opportunities and increasing household incomes (Cronin-Gilmore, 2012; U.S. Census Bureau, 2014). According to the U.S. Small Business Administration (2005), approximately 50% of starting small businesses ceased operations within the first 5 years (p. 1). Given the alarming small business closure of approximately 50% (Cronin-Gilmore, 2012, p. 96), a need existed to explore the factors that contributed to the failure of small businesses within five years of initial operations. The inability of small business owners to reduce business failure rates (U.S. Census Bureau, 2014, p. 1) generated an impetus for the researcher of the current study to produce reliable information that may be used in preventing failure of small businesses (Gary, 2013).

Leaders of global countries, such as the United States, supported small businesses in an attempt to prevent failure and drive the domestic economies (Adamoniene & Andriuscenka, 2007), which contributed primarily to the general economic growth and development (Lawrence, 2010; Singh, Garg, & Deshmukh, 2008). Longley (2009) concurred with the argument that country leaders promoted small businesses in response to the turbulent business environments that might lead to small business failure and need to foster competitive advantage, innovation and creativity, growth, and profitability strategies. Despite the significance of the small businesses in growing the economies, researchers provided statistics to show that small businesses were increasingly subjected to challenges in the past decade, leading to inconsistent failure rates and extinction (Discover the Network, 2011; U.S. Census Bureau, 2014). The current study involved interviewing owners of small businesses who experienced failure of small businesses. The participants were asked to describe lived experiences concerning the failure of their small businesses to allow a deeper understanding of the causes of failure of small businesses. Public records from the city of San Jose were used as a source to identify the owners of small businesses.

Included in Chapter 1 is an introduction of the research topic, a discussion of background information, and statements of the research problem and purpose. The importance of the current study findings to research and leadership followed. Also included is a discussion of the significance and nature of the research; the research and sub-research questions; the theoretical framework; definitions of important terms; and the scope, assumptions, limitations, delimitations of the study. The chapter ends with a summary. A qualitative phenomenological intrinsic study was conducted to examine the lived experiences of small business owners who experienced failure of small businesses to understand better the causes of failure of small businesses.

Background of the Problem

The author of the U.S. Census Bureau (2014) used statistics to indicate the overwhelming significance of small businesses in growing the U.S. economies. Despite the primary function of small businesses in generating employment opportunities and household incomes (Harold, Gurpreet, & Sajid, 2011), small businesses continued to fail at the rate of 50% before the fifth anniversary (Cronin-Gilmore, 2012, p. 96). Various factors contributed to the 50% failure rate of small businesses within 3 and 5 years of initial business operation (Lusky & Lusky, 2006, p. 1). Holland (1998, pp. 1-2) argued that only 1/2 of the small businesses that did not fail within the initial year of operation survived to their fifth anniversary. The key intellectual curiosity for the current study was to understand the inability of small businesses to maintain low failure rates. Scant empirical research existed on the failure of small businesses (Amel & Imen, 2012; Kamal, 2009; Will, 2008). However, the authors of existing studies recognized that small business owners continued to experience effects resulting from poor leadership practices at the global and regional levels, which resulted in failure (Beaver & Jennings, 2005; Divsalar, Firouzabadi, Sadeghi, Behrooz, & Alavi, 2011; Jui-Chen & Silverthorne, 2005).

Most organizational stakeholders applied the theory of strategic contingencies to explain proper leadership steps owner leaders of businesses needed to take to avoid failure of organizations and ultimately enhance successes (Ricardo Vinícius & de Souza, 2013). Ricardo Vinícius and de Souza (2013) argued that scholars used the theory of strategic contingencies to recognize the significance of leaders' capability to vary and apply suitable and effective leadership decision practices as necessitated by varied situations (Bass, 1990; Hersey & Blanchard, 1969; Lawrence, 2010; Newstrom & Davis, 2002; Ricardo Vinícius & de Souza, 2013). Organizational leaders may prevent failure of businesses by applying the flexibility principle of the theory of strategic contingencies (Bass, 1990; Hersey & Blanchard, 1969). Kamisan and King (2013) applauded the views of Bass (1990) and Hersey and Blanchard (1969) that the inability of leaders to establish a thriving culture within an organization might lead to failure. Kamisan and King (2013) argued that a culture that was supportive of employee relationships was necessary for an organization's prosperity.

According to Karanja et al. (2013), the owners of small businesses made the initial decisions that determined the success or failure of the small businesses. Furthermore, Karanja et al. (2013) argued that most small business owners did not comprehend the unique nature of small business leadership, which resulted in mismanagement of the business and ultimate failure. Researchers at Statistics Canada (1997) concurred with Karanja et al.'s (2013) and Brouthers, Gelderman, and Arens' (2007) argument that failure of small businesses was attributed by weak general leadership practices, which led to poor planning, marketing, and financial decisions.

Although Perry (2009) argued that environmental and other non-leadership factors, such as human and financial resource constraints, reduced share prices, limited access to funding or goods, and low investment returns might have contributed to failure of small businesses, quality leadership issues seemed to severely impact small businesses (Bernal, 1996; Will, 2008). Fink and Ploder (2009) argued that as leaders of small businesses, it was the responsibility of small business owners to provide the needed technical support. Reynolds (2010) agreed with Fink and Ploder's (2009) argument that small business owners engaged excessively in bureaucracy that adversely impacted small business. Reynolds (2010) asserted that small business owners' decisions resulted in resource misallocation and diversion of focus toward activities that did not promote competitive advantage and ulti-mately led to the failure of the small business. Taking bank credit at times of imperfect markets, accompanied with high interests charged to small business borrowers, results from poor leadership decisions, which adversely affects the sus-tainability of small businesses (Ganster, 2007; Zecchini & Ventura, 2009).

Reviewing the small business owners' description of the lived experiences concerning the failure of the small busi-nesses during the interview could offer insight into the factors that contributed to the failure of small businesses. The owners and leaders of small businesses may use the knowledge to avoid similar business practices that led to small business failure by enhancing proven small business competitive and sustaining strategies (Fisher, 2010). As leaders of small busi-nesses, owners need to support the business to attain competi-tive advantage by applying and sustaining core capabilities of proper leadership behavior such as; (a) team and group build-ing, (b) fostering good employee relationships, (c) construc-tively resolving internal conflicts, (d) encouraging and motivating stakeholders, (e) sound modeling, (f) facilitating and managing change, (g) maintaining low production cost, (h) seeking for new market opportunities, (i) developing inno-vative designs, and (j) maintaining high quality and original-ity of the product (Rabino, Simoni, & Zanni, 2008).

Small business organizations dominate economies of both developing and developed countries (Dobbs & Hamilton, 2007; Habaradas, 2008). Habaradas (2008) and Nguyen and Robinson (2010) argued that in the United States like in many developed countries, small businesses' challenges included limited (a) human and financial resources, (b) expertise and competence, and (c) business information access. The limitations pose dangers to small business sustainability, which lead to the trend of failure trend. To respond successfully to the market demands and sustainability, owners of small-scale businesses need to develop innovative project competencies and improve technology (Habaradas, 2008). The market demands include (a) intense competition, (b) need to adjust to customers' choices and profiles, and (c) the ability to provide improved quality at reduced costs (Habaradas, 2008), which small business owners must strive to attain to prevent the trend of failure.

In some U.S. economies, numerous leadership-related issues posed hindrances to the resilience and competitiveness of small business (Arasti, Zandi, & Talebi, 2012; Maryland Chamber of Commerce, 2004; Samad, Abdullah, Jusoff, Mohamad, & Nair, 2010). Poor leadership decision practices lead to (a) poor teams or group building, (b) unresolved conflicts among employees, (c) low employee morale and discouragement, (d) workplace dissatisfaction, (e) low workforce retention, (f) poor customer service and low returns, (g) difficulties in acquiring credit, (h) higher interests charged on loans, (i) shortage of human labor, (j) expensive to hire more competent and skilled labor , and (k) difficulties in accessing modern and most recent technology (Samad et al., 2010). Samad et al. argued that members of most governments did not seem to identify the necessary thriving strategies for small business owners' competitive advantage. When small business owners adopt successful strategies to struggling small businesses, their best practice and strategy efforts are not recognized (Gary, 2013). Gary (2013) argued that small business owners could take the initiative in gaining such recognition. The role of small business owners in improving the performance of the businesses is critical, and small business owners could not rely too much on government assistance for performance improvement (Samad et al., 2010).

Dasgupta and Sanyal (2010) asserted that failure was viewed to occur in a specific industry the business was operated based on the inability of the business to compete successfully in the industry. Some characteristics conspicuously dominant in certain industries, such as the construction and retail industries, do not allow the industries to continue competing successfully (Dasgupta & Sanyal, 2010). Despite the existing research and theories, identifying the major cause for the failure of small business was challenging, and even though failure continued to impact societies at broader levels, establishing a management theory to explain the predominant cause remains difficult (Nadim & Lussier, 2010).

Baron, Franklin, and Hmieleski, (2013) argued leaders may integrate suitable theories when making policies aimed at preventing failure of business. According to Baron et al., Successful leaders used decision-making strategies grounded in appropriate theories of management to guide the policy-making process. Nevertheless, leaders experience difficulties, such as identifying an appropriate theory of management to use in different situations (Robert et al., 2013).

The current phenomenological study could result in data

useful for extending the previous research focused on small business owners' leadership functions and practices. Expanding on the failed small businesses, the owners who solely make primary business leadership decisions may offer an alternative viewpoint on leadership by reexamining the existing leadership theories. Given that small business owners function as small business leaders, exploring the lived experiences of the failure of small businesses could result in a deeper understanding of the factors that contribute to the failure of small businesses and also optional information, behaviors, and skills necessary for small business success (Kouzes & Posner, 2012). Kouzes and Posner (2012) argued that organizational leaders avoided failure when they set the best example (model), inspired others toward a common vision, took initiative for new opportunities as a way of challenging the process, empowered others, and motivated and encouraged others through recognition and appreciation of achievements.

Problem Statement

The general problem is the high failure rates of small businesses in the United States, and the alarming trend may continue to affect the U.S. economy adversely despite the significance of the small businesses (U.S. Small Business Administration, 2011). Although the place of small businesses in the U.S. economy was invaluable—generated approximately 75% new employment opportunities, constituted 95% of employers (U.S. Census Bureau, 2014, p. 1), and used to enhance household incomes, small businesses continued to fail at the rate of 50% before the fifth anniversary (Cronin-Gilmore, 2012, p. 96; Yallapragada & Bhuiyan, 2011, p. 117).

Cronin-Gilmore (2012), as well as Yallapragada and Bhuiyan (2011), argued that leadership problems certainly caused the failing trend more than non-leadership factors. The U.S. economy included 23 million small businesses (Cronin-Gilmore, 2012, p. 96), and small businesses accounted for 54% of all U.S. sales (U.S. Census Bureau, 2014, p. 1). A large portion of small business owners occupying the U.S. economy contributed approximately 39% of the gross domestic product and created two-thirds of job opportunities (Yallapragada & Bhuiyan, 2011, p. 117). Furthermore, a review of studies revealed that small businesses primarily contributed to the countries' economic growth (Singh et al., 2008) as the businesses continued to drive domestic economies (Adamoniene & Andriuscenka, 2007). Lack of action to address the failure of small businesses will become detrimental to the U.S. economy (Yallapragada & Bhuiyan, 2011).

The specific problem was to uncover the predominant cause of failure of small businesses (San Jose City, 2013). Existing small business owners need assistance in identifying and addressing potential causes of business failure before escalating to foreclosure. One would question the inability of 50% small business owners to sustain low failure rates in the United States (Cronin-Gilmore, 2012, p. 96).

San Jose, in particular, had an increased number of small business closures resulting from lack of both entrepreneurial activities and productivity (City of San Jose, 2013) to generate the economy (Longley, 2009; Reynolds, 2010; Tambunan, 2008). In 2003, 25,400 jobs were lost in San Jose compared to 36,200 in 2009 (EDD and California Department of Finance, 2010, p. 15), which accounted for 53% of the Santa Clara County population and accounted for 42% of the job base in 2003. In 2009, the population of San Jose was 54% of Santa Clara County with a 40% job base ((EDD and California Department of Finance, 2010, p. 15).

The intellectual curiosity for the current study was the inability of the small business owners' leadership behavior to maintain the low failure rates gained in 2003 (EDD and California Department of Finance, 2010). A review of most existing research indicated no clear predominant cause for the failure of small businesses (Aterido, Hallward-Driemeier, & Pages, 2011; Rogoff, Lee, & Suh, 2004). Aterido et al. (2011) indicated that factors not related to leadership, such as economics and politics, might have contributed to the failure of small businesses. Nevertheless, Shiladitya and Debashish (2010) argued that ineffective small business leadership practices inevitably led to failure. Small business owners solely made decisions for the businesses (Karanja et al., 2013).

The researcher used a purposive sample of small business owners who experienced failure of small businesses to explore the causes of the phenomenon of small business failure using the lived experiences. Exploring the lived experiences of small business owners who experienced failure of small businesses could lead to increased understanding of the failure of small businesses and offer insight on the causes of small business failure. The owner leaders of existing small businesses could use the knowledge to avoid similar experiences by upholding small business thriving leadership behaviors needed to prevent the occurrence of the phenomenon of small business failure causing severe unemployment in and impacting the US economy adversely.

Purpose Statement

A qualitative phenomenological intrinsic study was used to explore lived experiences of owners of small businesses who experienced failure to understand the causes of failure of small businesses (San Jose City, 2013). In the study, failure of businesses was used to refer to termination of operations to avoid further losses to owner leaders and shareholders (Hunter, 2011). Hunter (2011) argued that the inability of owner leaders of small businesses to generate profits or enough income to meet the expenses resulted in failure. Owner leaders of small businesses who experienced failure of small businesses were asked to describe the meaning of the lived experiences to gain a better understanding of the pre-dominant causes of small business failure (San Jose City, 2013).

Researchers used qualitative methodologies to enhance the insight of individuals' experiences with phenomena, especially the ones with minimal existing information ("Snap Surveys Ltd.," 2009; Strauss & Corbin, 1990). In the study, ten small business owners were asked to describe the lived experiences concerning the failure of their small businesses. Small business owners made primary decisions for the business (Karanja et al., 2013) and examined the lived experiences of small business owners who experienced failure could help to uncover the causes of the phenomenon (Moustakas, 1994) of failure of small businesses. The main process of collecting data involved telephone and in-depth personal interviews with a purposive sample of voluntary participants.

The public records kept and maintained by the City of San Jose Department of Commerce, and Economic Planning were used to identify and locate the research participants to be interviewed. The selected participants must have possessed lived experiences of the phenomenon of failure of small businesses. Small business failure in the current research referred to the termination of business operations or closure to avoid organizational bankruptcy or fiscal and monetary losses (Headd, 2003; Hunter, 2011). Furthermore, the current study was used to pay particular attention to the phenomenon of small business failure.

Significance of Study

A review of existing literature indicated the lack of a primary factor contributing to the failure of small businesses (Rogoff et al., 2004). The importance of small businesses in driving the U.S. economy, the alarming failure rates, and nonexistence of causes of failure (Ibrahim, Angelidis, & Parsa, 2004) necessitated an investigative research to understand the failure of small businesses. Describing the lived experiences concerning the failure of small businesses could result in identifying and better understanding of the predominant causes of failure of small businesses and seek for solutions to prevent adverse domestic and national economic consequences.

The current study may help to narrow the likely factors

that cause the failure of small businesses and add the findings to the research field. According to Creswell (2007), adequate knowledge enhanced the understanding of a research problem. Adequate information may allow small business owners and leaders to avoid similar practices by generating rational decision practices (Avolio & Yammarino, 2013; Kouzes & Posner, 2012) known for preventing the failures of small businesses (Storey, 1994). The current study involved examining characteristics of small business failure.

Small businesses foreclosure rates in is adversely affecting employment opportunities and sustainability of a productive economy. The current study's findings may provide knowledge to guide future researchers regarding the failure of small businesses. According to Creswell (2007), research was significant when it contributed to the existing body of knowledge in the field. The significant role played by small businesses in providing employment and developing the U.S. economy necessitates future research be focused on examining the factors that cause failure of small businesses (Beaver, 2003). The causes will be used in formulating better failure preventive measures.

Significance of the Study to Leadership. The current study may contribute significantly to the entrepreneurial information leaders may use to avoid similar leadership practices that led to the failure of small businesses and seek for proper leadership behaviors known to sustain business organizations (Avolio & Yammarino, 2013; Kouzes & Posner, 2012; McKinney, 2009). Small business leaders may utilize the current study's findings to improve the resilience and responsiveness of business organizations in difficult business surroundings (Sooksan, 2009). Also, organizational leaders and entrepreneurs apply the results of the current study to develop successful tactics and policies that support funding (Arasti et al., 2012), to enhance performance in entrepreneurship and human resources practices (Yu, 2010), and to achieve sustainability and prevent the decline and failure of small businesses (Bandi & Lefter, 2009).

Owner-leaders of small businesses may also use the results of the current study to seek for alternative improved leadership decision-making skills and develop responsible organizational cultures aimed at avoiding failure of small business organizations (Avolio & Yammarino, 2013; Kouzes & Posner, 2012). To achieve this goal, Tseng (2010) concurred with the view of Avolio and Yammarino (2013) and Kouzes and Posner (2012) that the owners of small businesses needed to establish effective and responsive leadership strategies for their small businesses to successfully overcome current and future difficult business environments. Moreover, the results may also help small business leaders to determine market demands and opportunities through an amalgamation of creative thinking, superior management capability and resource allocations, and close monitoring of the market trend or environment (Yu, 2010).

In the current research, small business leaders and entrepreneurs may gain new informational insight concerning causes that contribute to increasing failure rate trend of small businesses and search for (a) ways to prevent failure of small businesses and continue business improvement and sustainability and (b) new alternative funding methods to triumph over financing intricacies (Yu, 2010). The study may add new information that may be used to add investment opportunities via the organizational vision, such as developing of realistic innovation, real business strategy, and business intelligence (Kantabutra, 2009). Applying new information to the business leadership and management field will significantly contribute toward finding solutions to business problems through logical truth and methods (Helsinki University of Technology, 2008). From the current study, small business leaders may gain information required for developing commitment to learning of organizations, instituting transformations in leadership and culture, and implementing the strategies and practices needed to solve or alleviate business challenges (Avolio & Yammarino, 2013; Kouzes & Posner, 2012) and prevent small business failure (Karanja et al., 2013).

Significant information and other secondary sources textbooks existed in the area of business failure (Amel & Akkari, 2012; Hunter, 2011; Schehr, 2011). However, a lack of phenomenological exploration existed on the topic of the small business failure (Arasti et al., 2012; Liao, Welsch, & Moutray, 2009). Moreover, limited research existed on small business failure about San Jose, California. The current study's findings may contribute new information that small businesses leaders might use to avoid the same trend of small business failure (Maryland Chamber of Commerce, 2004). According to members of the Maryland Chamber of Commerce (2004), leaders might use the vital knowledge of the small business failure to increase their understanding of the meaning small business owners attach to the predominant cause of small business failure as they describe their lived experiences concerning the failure of small businesses.

Nature of the Study

Researchers used qualitative (Gaskill, Van Auken, & Manning, 1993), quantitative (Edmister, 1972), and mixed-method approaches (Gaskill et al., 1993) to examine the factors causing the failures of small businesses. The nature of the information sought for becomes the guiding principle for any researcher in selecting the best methodology to use in a study (Collins, 2003). The current study involved focusing on gaining a better understanding of the predominant cause of failure of the small business.

Research Method: A qualitative phenomenological intrinsic study was used to explore lived experiences of small business owners who experienced failure understand the failure of small businesses (San Jose City, 2013). Qualitative Method used allowed one to gain a broader perception of the problem examined (Creswell, 2012; Moustakas, 1996). A study involving a qualitative method required the continuous gathering of the data (Byrne, 2009; Creswell et al., 2010). Qualitative Method was used to explore numerous possibilities to approach the research problem (Creswell, 2012).

The lived experiences of small business owners who experienced failure of small businesses was used to enhance an understanding of the predominant factors contributing to failure of small businesses, leading to foreclosure and affecting adversely the U.S economy (San Jose City, 2013). The sectors included (a) recreational, (b) wholesale and retail, (c) service,

(d) construction, (e) housing and f) transportation and communications. At least, one member from each of the seven sectors participated in interviews. Through cultural immersion, the qualitative research method led to direct researcher-participant interaction and perceptual data (Weinreich, 2006).

In the current study, a qualitative phenomenological intrinsic design using a modified van Kaam approach was applied to gain an in-depth understanding of the occurrence of the phenomenon (Moustakas, 1996). The structured approach was to gain a better understanding of the problem that entailed elimination of the previous judgments or assumptions and concentrating in acquiring clear and bias-free findings (Blum & Muirhead, 2005; Moustakas, 1994). According to Moustakas (1994), the modified van Kaam approach involved the following specific steps for analyzing the data:

1. Preliminary listing and grouping.
2. Reduction and exclusion.
3. Invariant constituent clustering or grouping and thematization.
4. Constituent (invariant) identification and theme application.
5. Textural description of each participant's lived experience, applying relevant variant constituents and themes.
6. Structural experience construction for every individual co-researcher was relying on personal variations in imaginations and textural descriptions.
7. Textural structure construction for every research participant, describing the meanings and significance of lived experiences.
8. Constituent (variant) and theme integration. (pp. 121-122)

The usefulness of qualitative research included allowing one to understand the fundamental basis of a phenomenon, provided insights to the problem background, generated ideas and hypotheses that could undergo quantitative testing, and discover general trends in perceptions (Creswell, 2012; Creswell, Hanson, Plano Clark, & Morales, 2007; "Snap Surveys Ltd," 2009). The qualitative method was suitable for the current study because the approach was used to achieve the goal of exploring a phenomenon (Creswell, 2005; Creswell et al., 2007; Wojnar & Swanson, 2007). Researchers use qualitative methods to understand the mental processes affecting conscious or unconscious behaviors and participants' viewpoints (Creswell et al., 2007). The current study involved using a qualitative method to produce richer and more detailed data than a quantitative method (Creswell, 2010; Weinreich, 2006).

Research Questions

The purpose the qualitative phenomenological study was to understand the failure of small businesses (San Jose City, 2013). Exploring the lived experiences of small business owners who experienced failure of small businesses may result in a better understanding of the predominant causes of failure of small businesses (San Jose City, 2013) and impacting the U.S. economy (U.S. Small Business Administration, 2011) adversely. In the current study, the researcher used phenomenological research questions to ascertain the core experience of every study participant concerning the essential phenomenon of failure of a small business (Creswell et al., 2007).

Aligned with the purpose of the research to examine the central phenomenon of failure of small businesses, the main research question (RQ) used to guide the current study was; how do small business owners who experienced failure perceive and interpret the meaning of the lived experiences?

The central research question was used to focus on eliciting small business owner-leaders' lived experiences of failure of small business. The goal was not to identify relationships among variables or examine trends but explore the central phenomenon to gain a better understanding of how small business owner-leaders who experienced failure of small businesses perceived and described the lived experiences with causes of the central phenomenon of business failure (Bloomberg & Volpe, 2008; Neuman, 2005). When performing a qualitative research, researcher used sub-research questions to increase the understanding of a central phenomenon (Creswell, 2005).

The following sub-research questions supported the study's main research question:
- What is the perception and interpretation of small business owners who experienced failure about the unique features contributing to the failure of small businesses?
- What is the perception and interpretation of small business owners who experienced failure about leadership causing failure of small businesses?
- How do small business owners who experienced failure perceive and interpret non-leadership factors, such as business location, and size contributing to the failure of small businesses?

The focus of first sub-research question was on the perception of the unique features representing common elements of
the small business entity that could lead to failure. The second sub-research question was focused on the perception of
the leadership decision-making inabilities contributing to the
failure of the small businesses. The third sub-research question was used to focus on the perception of non-leadership related causes, such as organizational location, size, and
planning contributed to the failure of small businesses.

Theoretical Framework

The organizational leadership process required the ability
of leaders to optimize the followers' performance in an organization (Shultz, 2003). Many scholars argue the application of
the theory of strategic contingencies results in optimizing
workforce productivity in businesses (Bass, 1990; Hersey &
Blanchard, 1969; Newstrom & Davis, 2002). Scholars used
research to indicate that managers need to perform operational tasks efficiently for organizations to achieve specific
goals (Wren, 1994).

The review of the primary features of the theory of strategic contingencies indicated that for the best results, leaders
needed to vary their practices and behaviors as necessitated
by an organization's specific operational conditions (Bass,
1990; Hersey & Blanchard, 1969; Newstrom & Davis, 2002).
In the current study, the theory of strategic contingencies was
applicable because researchers in the previous studies interrelated failures of small businesses to the aspects of leadership and management behaviors (Bouchikhi, 1993; Hersey &

Blanchard, 1969). The findings of the present study may increase the understanding of causes of failure of small business and may be used to improve the areas of leadership and theory of management. Research in the areas of management theory and leadership may be used to focus on improving the performance of organizations by weighing in the skills pertaining leadership and management (Briggs, 2013; Ellis, 2012; Wren, 1994). Improved theories of management and leadership may be used to focus on identifying suitable leadership and managerial practices to enhance the performance of employees and overall organizations (Briggs, 2013; Ellis, 2012; Maryland Chamber of Commerce, 2004; Wren, 1994).

The purpose of the prior studies was to enhance an understanding of the causes that resulted in failure of small businesses. However, the review of the previous research was focused on various circumstances to establish the causes of failure of the small businesses (Beaver, 2003; Bouchikhi, 1993; Campbell, 2004; Tuleasca, 2012). The objective was to incorporate specific issues related to small businesses, improve leadership behaviors and the theory of management (Tuleasca, 2012), and assist in minimizing failure of small businesses.

Definitions of Terms

Following are definitions of terms critical to the current study:

Small business. Many scholars define small business in different ways. Some defined small business as any organization bearing the name of the owner, place of business operation, and one or more employees (Karanja et al., 2013; Kobe, 2007a; Tate, Megginson, Scott & Trueblood, 1978; Yallapragada & Bhuiyan, 2011). Others viewed small business as any organization operated by three or fewer managers or with fewer than 100 employees (City of San Jose, 2013; Hertz, 1982; Kobe, 2007b; Peterson, Albaum, & Kozmetsky, 1986). For the purpose of the present study, small business refers to independently owned and operated organizations with either up to a maximum of 100 workers or $1 million gross revenue investment (City of San Jose, 2013).

Failure. Gary (2013) defined failure as insolvency and bankruptcy of business (Ong, Yap, & Khong, 2011), lack of funds (Richardson et al., 1994), and defaulting of business (Tserng, Liao, Tsai, & Chen, 2011). For the purpose of the current study, failure refers to termination (Russell & Zhai, 1996) or ceasing of business operations (BusinessDictionary.com, 2014) because of liquidation issues (Morris, 1997) to avoid future loss of finance (Gary, 2013).

Business failure. Business failure was used for business termination or discontinuation for various reasons causes (Hussain, Si, Xie, & Wang, 2010). Bankruptcy. When a person or business entity is legally unable to repay debts owed (Carmen et al., 2009).

Sustainability. According to LandLearn NSW (2010), sustainability was used to refer to the capacity of business to maintain itself. In the current study, sustainability was used to mean successful maintenance of the business.

Small business owner. For the current study, small business owner-leader refers to the person solely responsible for making significant decisions for the small business. The term is used interchangeably with the small business leader (Gary, 2013).

Assumptions

In the current qualitative phenomenological study, it was assumed the researcher remained unbiased when interviewing, and the research participants responded candidly and honestly to the interview questions. Dishonest responses would lead to incorrect describing of the lived experiences of the phenomena by participants, and this would adversely influence the analysis and understanding of the data.

For the purpose of the current study, the physical location where to conduct face-to-face interviews was assumed to be available and there was no need for making prior visits to the interview location. Moreover, the location was assumed to be convenient for interviewing and secure to protect the participant's identities.

It was assumed that technology was static or non-existent. However, doing business through Internet and Online continue to change the way businesses are done. Location does not influence most current businesses (Shaoming et al., 2009).

The category of population sample used was assumed to be representative. Small business owners who experienced failure were assumed to proportionately represent gender and age (Neuman, 2006).

Scope

The current qualitative phenomenological study was used to focus on exploring the central phenomena of failure of small businesses to gain a better understanding of the principal cause of the occurrence. The scope of the current study was limited to the insights concerning the failure of ten small businesses. Perception included that the ten research participants would not limit the explorations of how organizational leadership and non-leadership aspects such as organizational size, location, and planning could affect the sustainability of sectors of small business enterprises in San Jose localities or markets.

Limitations

Limitations were used to refer to the potential indicators of weaknesses demonstrated in a study (Creswell, 2005). One of the limitations of the current study was the participants' interpretation of the phenomenon. A possibility existed that participants could be unwilling, un-open, and dishonest, which could affect the accuracy of the information gathered as the in-depth of interviewing depends on participants' honesty. Furthermore, the participants could exhibit failure in recalling events connected to the study during interviewing.

Bias of the researcher could be another limitation to the current study. In the current study, the researcher functioned as the primary investigator and instrument of the study. The researcher had no previous experience or background concerning the failure of small businesses. Another potential limitation included the researcher's influence on the participants during interviewing. The researchers' ability to append or influence any prior perceptions or information about the phenomenon, so as to gather unbiased information, would have been another limitation of the current study.

The purposive method of sampling, a type of nonrandom participant selection, was a study limitation. The study utilized the purposive method to select the samples from well-developed San Jose localities--10 small business owners from the six sectors of (a) recreational, (b) wholesale and retail, (c) service, (d) construction, (e) housing, and (f) transportation and communications. The purposive method of sampling involved selecting potential participants for a specific purpose, instead of selecting randomly (Creswell, 2005, 2007; Neuman, 2005).

Delimitations

Scholars used delimitations to refer to the factors used to restrict and narrow a study (Creswell, 2005; Leedy & Ormrod, 2005). In the current study, the selected population was limited to owners of small businesses in San Jose, California that limited enormously the capacity to the generalization of the results. The small business population, which operated with a maximum of 100 workers, would not limit the generalization ability of businesses with similar sizes. The inability of the researcher to ascertain sincere responses of the participants was delimitation. Comprehending the causes of failures of small businesses depended on sincere responses of each small business owner, which was also an assumption of the current study.

Selecting two small business owners from each of the six sectors was delimitation. The target population for the current study was small business owners with up to 100 workers, who operated a small business for five years and failed. The purpose of the current study was to explore the lived experiences of owners of small businesses who experienced failure to increase an understanding of the causes of the phenomena.

Summary

The purpose of the study was to explore the lived experiences of small business owners who experienced small business failure to increase understanding of the predominant cause. Chapter 1 included an introduction and background of the current study. The chapter included discussion of the argument that the inability of the small business owners to sustain the businesses generated the need for the study. Persistent failure rates of small businesses pose a leadership predicament when generating the policies aimed at sustaining low failure rates. A large portion of the U.S. economy is supported by small businesses, and putting in place the policies to prevent small business failure may help to reverse the adverse economic consequences (U.S. Small Business Administration, 2005).

Chapter 1 was also used to cover a discussion of the problem and purpose statements, significance, and nature of the study. Although other methods of research exist, such as quantitative and mixed-methods, the qualitative method was most appropriate because of the alignment with the purpose of the study to understand the failure of small businesses (Edmister, 1972; Gaskill et al., 1993). Furthermore, included in Chapter 1 was a discussion of the study research questions; the theoretical framework; definitions of terms; and the study assumptions, scope, limitations, and delimitations.

Chapter 2 follows with an in-depth presentation of the available literature review used to detail the factors that contributed to the failure of small businesses. The literature review originated from articles, searches, journals, books used to expand the research objectives, and documents from prior research. Also presented in Chapter 2 is the historical overview used to explain possible causes of failure of small businesses. Included in Chapter 2 discussion is the literature gaps from the previous studies.

Chapter 2
Review of the Literature

In the present study, a qualitative method was selected because the method would be used to offer a unique understanding of the factors that contributed to the failure of small businesses.

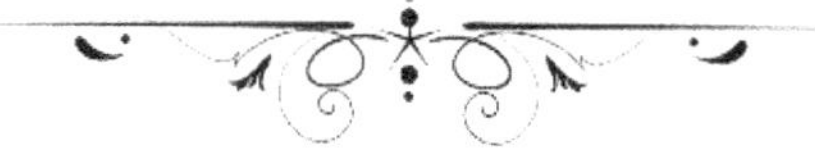

The purpose of the current study was to explore the lived experiences of small business owners concerning the failure of small businesses to understand the causes of increasing failure rate trend of small businesses. Chapter 2 was used to provide a review of literature. The review of literature included germinal literature searches to provide the research background and framework. Also literature gaps concerning failure of small businesses are identified in the Chapter.

Moreover, peer-reviewed literature was scarce during the current study to be used for consultancy of small business owners.

Chapter 2 was used to expand the scarce empirical research on the primary cause for the occurring of the phenomenon. Included in the chapter is the information about sources accessed to gather pertinent information on the research topic. The historical overview on the failure of small businesses was presented as the foundation on the topic and the direction of the research to the reader. Chapter 2 includes an in-depth literature review of the possible causes of failure of a small business.

In the discussion, literature from the divergent viewpoints describing the failure of small businesses was reviewed following a general to the specific strategy. The sections of Chapter 2 included (a) title searches, articles, research documents, and journals; (b) historical overview; (c) literature gaps; (d) empirical research; (e) research methodology and design; and (f) the summary and conclusion. Knowledge gained from the discussion was used to attain a better understanding of the development of the causes of failure of small businesses.

The data gathering method in the current study involved in-depth telephone and personal interviews with a purposive sample of voluntary participants. Having direct lived experiences in the failure of small business was to be used to form the criteria for selecting the current study participants. The public records of owners of small business kept and maintained by the city of San Jose city was used as a reliable source for identifying and locating the study participants for interviewing. Failure of business was used to refer to the terminating of organization's operations to avoid either bankruptcy or loss of finances (Headd, 2003; Robert et al., 2013; Tuleasca, 2012; Ucbasaran, Shepard, Lockett, & Lyon, 2013).

Title Searches, Articles, Research Documents, Journals

Searches for literature was used to reveal peer-reviewed journal articles on topics associated with key topics of the current study, such as poor leadership of small business (a) location (b) size, (c) planning, and (d) leadership. The literature review is the representation of not only germinal literature related to the failure of small businesses but also existing literature. Literature reviewed was used to build a foundation for the theoretical framework for the current study and entailed different author's viewpoints on relevant topics. Moreover, through the review of the literature, gaps in the literature concerning the unsustainability of small businesses were revealed.

The sources included in the literature review were (a) published peer-reviewed articles; (b) completed and approved dissertations; (c) scholarly books, articles, and journals; (d) reports maintained by state, federal, and other governmental organizations or agencies; e) the University of Phoenix online scholarly books; and (f) periodicals. The literature search process was used to assist in establishing an in-depth understanding of available historical and current knowledge from the approved databases of ProQuest Dissertations and Theses and EBSCOHost. The parameter used to guide the searches confined the current study to the peer-reviewed sources only (Mannelly, 2009).

Historical Perspective

A wide-ranging historical perspective was used as the foundation for the literature that centered on causes of failure of small businesses (Adam & Sykes, 2003; Arinaitwe, 2006; Beaver, 2003; Bouchikhi, 1993; Edmister, 1972; Kline, 1974; Perry, 2002; Rogoff et al., 2004). Kline (1974) emphasized on the factors that caused failure of small businesses and made many of conclusions concerning the causes, such as managerial and decision-making inabilities. Although based on the previous empirical study, Edmister's (1972) analysis associated the factor of finances with leadership and managerial shortcomings to predict failure of small businesses(Dasgupta & Sanyal, 2010).

Scholars of the studies who explored the causes of small business failure cited leadership deficiencies or inabilities repeatedly as the cause of the failure of small businesses (Audretsch, 2012; Darling & Leffel, 2010; Hunter, 2011). However, researchers of many other studies identified the factor of financing as the cause of failure of small businesses, excluding management and leadership inabilities (Ganster, 2007; Gary, 2013). Ganster (2007) and Gary (2013) concluded that difficulties related to funding contributed to the failure of small businesses.

Audretsch (2012) advanced the previous studies to examine the failure of small businesses. Audretsch (2012) concurred largely with Kline (1974), who identified the inability of managers as the key contributing factor for small business failure. Gaskill et al. (1993) explored a small retail enterprise in Iowa to understand the unique nature of the problem of the study the failure of small businesses. Numerous wider perspectives of the issue of failure of small business emerged from a variety of analyses (Edmister, 1972; Gaskill et al., 1993). Gaskill et al. (1993) persisted that scholars of prior research failed to identify a principal cause for the failure of small businesses. The results garnered from Gaskill et al.'s (1993) study were used to increase the understanding of the failure of small businesses, which in turn may be used to direct the future focus upon the knowledge related to the factors that contribute to the failure of small businesses.

Impact of Small Businesses

The role of small business enterprises in contributing to the gross domestic product is fundamental to the U.S. economy (Cronin-Gilmore, 2012). Small business owners contributed toward the large production levels in the private industry (Arasti et al., 2012; Heady et al., 2005). U.S leaders used small business enterprise to generate 97% of total U.S. exports and over half of the employment opportunities in the private industries (Cronin-Gilmore, 2012, p. 96; U.S. Small Business Administration, 2005, p. 1). At least 23 million small businesses operated in the United States (Cronin-Gilmore, 2012, p. 96; Heady, Maples, & Greco, 2005; Kobe, 2007a). The role of small businesses was used to reinforce the significance of the enterprises in future success of the U.S.

economy and increasing failure rates impact adversely the market operations, employment and societal living standards (Arasti et al., 2012; Cronin-Gilmore, 2012; Heady et al., 2005). The phenomenon is important to the policy-makers and owners of future small businesses based on the extensive functions of small business in the economy (Arasti et al., 2012).

Although the stakeholders take credit for putting in place policies that prevent the failure of small businesses, understanding the distinctive nature of the small business enterprises remains challenging (Teng, Bhatia, & Anwar, 2011). Teng et al. (2011) recommended that researchers needed to conduct studies focused on specific issues that uniquely used to define small businesses. In agreement, Bouchikhi (1993) and Hunter (2011) indicated that information about the failure of small businesses was limited. The authors' arguments led to information that may be used for partial understanding of the incoherent failure rates experienced by small businesses (City of San Jose, 2013; U.S. Small Business Administration, 2005).

In the study, the Theory of Strategic Contingencies was used in an attempt to address the central phenomenon and prevent it from occurring, which supported efforts aimed at avoiding the failure of organizations (Johnson, 2014; Karanja et al., 2013; Kayemuddin, 2012; Liao et al., 2009). The Theory of Strategic Contingencies was operated on the premise that leaders demonstrated the ability to apply proper leadership behaviors as required by the situation (Johnson, 2014; Kayemuddin, 2012; Liao et al., 2009). Aterido et al. (2011)

and Campbell (2004) deviated slightly on the significance of leadership in dealing with the failure of organizations. Instead of focusing on the appropriate leadership behavior and practices to avoid organizational failure, Aterido at el. (2011) advocated for leaders' abilities to generate successive cultures within organizations that would be used to promote good workforce relationships. Although the existing theories related closely to the efforts to prevent failure of businesses, obscurity continues to exist concerning the principal cause for the business failure (Gary, 2013), validating the need for further understanding of the problem.

Failure Rates and Small Businesses

Small businesses increasingly failed at higher rates than well-established and larger organizations (Hunter, 2011). The increasing failure rates of the small businesses continue to be the main focus of policies used to revitalize small businesses (Arasti et al., 2012; Holt, 2013). There is a huge concern for the existence of multiple definitions provided for small business failure (Fredland & Morris, 1976). However, the argument advanced for the existence of numerous definitions for small business failure was that scholars of the studies recognized divergent meanings based on the intended purpose of a specific study (Lussier & Halabi, 2010). Moreover, there exists incomplete information used primarily in the definition of failure, which results in misleading information about failure rates of small business (Beaver, 2003; McCartan-Quinn & Carson, 2003; Nadim & Lussier, 2010; Stokes & Blackburn, 2002).

The misleading knowledge about failure rate for small businesses not only results from using inappropriate information sources for failure rates but also from lack of current studies on the failure of small businesses (Schehr, 2011). When researchers used the collected data in the studies from sources intended for other purposes to explore small business failure, the likelihood of attaining misleading causes for failure of small businesses increased (Beaver, 2003; Nadim & Lussier, 2010; Schehr, 2011). Moreover, in an attempt to define the failure of small businesses, researchers used different categories or criterion, such as solvency, earnings, bankruptcy, and loss (Gary, 2013).

Common Definitions of Failure

Defining and understanding the central phenomenon of failure was the basis for the current study. The scope in defining failure can immensely impact the study findings (Schehr, 2011). Gary (2013) recognized that there were benefits and disadvantages of every definition applied to failure in attempting to gain a better understanding of the central phenomenon about the failure of small businesses. Defining failure is critical to filtering the collected data (Gary, 2013). The information used in multiple definitions of failure affected the understanding of the failure of small businesses (Nadim & Lussier, 2010; Schehr, 2011).

In the studies where failure was frequently discussed, most scholars often included termination of the business in the definition to avoid the losses to shareholders and creditors (Arasti et al., 2012; Gary, 2013; Liao et al., 2009). Although

Gary (2013) focused mainly on the criterion of solvency to define failure, using the solvency criterion in defining failure necessitated the inclusion of two conditions to define adequately business failure: (a) bankruptcy declaration by an organization and (b) possessing either unpaid promissory and obligations or losses incurred by the creditors (Gary, 2013).

In the discussion, Gary (2013) indicated that defining failure involved three categories: earnings, bankruptcy, and loss. The criterion of earnings was used to compare similar gains from investments. The failure occurred when gains on a specified investment resulted in significant and consistent lower revenue (Arasti et al., 2012; Gary, 2013; Liao et al., 2009; Ooghe & De Prijcker, 2008). The bankruptcy criterion was used to define failure from the legal perspective of bankruptcy declaration (Gary, 2013; Tuleasca, 2012). The criterion of loss was used to refer failure to an organization's termination of its operation to prevent further or marginal losses from the present financial position (Arasti et al., 2012; Gary, 2013; Liao et al., 2009; Ooghe & De Prijcker, 2008).

Cochran (1981) differed with prior scholars concerning the definition of failure. Cochran argued that failure described the inability of an organization to "make a go of it" (p. 52). Cochran stated that the inability of an organization's operations to remain competitive led to failure. The deviation entirely in definition from the four described criterion or categories creates a need for a distinct category that caters to the performance of an organization as it pertains to the competitors. Although the existing literature resulted in an incomplete, imprecise, and insufficient definition of failure, the available definitions were vital in forming a guiding framework for shaping the meaning of failure of small businesses for the purpose of the current study.

Analysis of Failure Definitions and Literature

Altman (1983) and Amel and Akkari (2012) used the concept of investment profits as a foundation for a variety of failure definitions--placing greater emphasis on the earnings. Definitions based on profits sent misleading information because organizations continued executing their operations even when investments yielded poor performances (Amel & Akkari, 2012; Gary, 2013). Dasgupta and Sanyal (2010) argued that defining failure using earnings excluded the malpractices of the owners of small businesses such as the unwillingness to report their financial information detailing performances, evading taxation, and employing archaic procedures of accounting (Arasti et al., 2012; Collis & Jarvis, 2002; Gary, 2013; Ooghe & De Prijcker, 2008; Storey, Keasey, Watson, & Wynarczyk, 1987).

Scholars associated the other three categories used to define failure with the flaws of the vulnerability of uncertainty because one needs an indefinable set of data to when using the categories to define failure adequately (Haswell & Holmes, 1989).

Recognizing the flaws in different definitions of failure increases the understanding of every possible interpretation. Multiple definitions of failure impact significantly the understanding of the general problem of small business failure

(Nadim & Lussier, 2010). Nadim and Lussier (2010) argued that lack of a universally applied definition, as it pertained to the business failure, undermined the analysis of data for small business failure.

An analysis of literature was used to indicate numerous inconsistencies concerning the failure of small businesses as it related closely to the issue of defining of failure (Amel & Akkari, 2012; Gary, 2013). The researchers argued that various scholars used previous data on the failure of small business to define the failure of small business variedly. Scholars of numerous studies exploring the failure of small businesses argued that defining failure of small businesses using the existing data generated a basis of inconsistency for determining the proper definition of failure, which clouded the understanding of the problem (Dasgupta & Sanyal, 2010; Gary, 2013). The continued lack of data regarding the failure of small businesses allowed researchers to alter consistently the meaning of failure based on the purpose of their studies (Dasgupta & Sanyal, 2010). Cochran (1981) analyzed and confirmed the impression that employing various sets of data to support the definitions of failure presented contradictory results to the researchers. Cochran (1981) argued that studies centered on the problem of the failure of small businesses resulted in conflicting messages or "speak to the subject with a babble of tongues" (p. 59). Cochran's (1981) statement was a confirmation of the non-existence of a universally accepted definition of failure (Arasti et al., 2012; Gary, 2013; Ooghe, & De Prijcker, 2008).

The current study was used to endeavor in integrating a meaning of failure to encompass the unique features of the central phenomenon as explained in existing studies. Blending the following two categories was used to define the unique aspect of failure: (a) the criterion of bankruptcy and (b) the criterion of loss (Gary, 2013). Recognizing the suitable set of data to fit the definition of failure was not only sufficient but also enhanced the rigor of the current study. Weighing on the experiences of the previous studies allowed the use of the definition of failure in the context of the current study and could be used to offer excellent information about the failure of small business enterprises to the future researchers.

Failure Defined and Context of Study

In the definitions, Arasti et al. (2012), Headd (2003), Liao et al. (2009), and Ooghe and De Prijcker (2008) viewed small business failure as the process that involved the transfer of business ownership to minimize losses in finance, closures, and bankruptcy. The definition applied in the current study did not include closures, as doing so would lead to focusing on owners of small businesses seeking to increase profits and evade failure. Integrating closures in defining of failure would necessitate managing non-financial intents resulting in operational termination (Arasti et al., 2012).

Examination of the failure and success of small businesses was used to show that a small number of business operation closures resulted from bankruptcy (Arasti et al., 2012; Beaver, 2003; Gary, 2013; Liao et al., 2009; Ooghe & De Prijcker, 2008). Arasti et al. (2012) argued that although financial factors partially resulted in closures, other factors played a more significant role. Exclusion of closures from the definition of failure of small businesses allowed the current study to be focused on the financial related distress only.

Small Business Failure and Understanding of Causes

The factors that contributed to the failure of small businesses varied remarkably as numerous researchers provided different causes, such as difficulties in financing, level of business maturity, and issues related to inefficient planning and management (Audretsch, 2012; Darling & Leffel, 2010; Gary, 2013; Gibb & Webb, 1980; Hunter, 2011; Skeete et al., 2008; Stanford, 1982). Nadim and Lussier (2010) affirmed the fact that the chances of small business failure were greatest within four years of business initiation. Small businesses that survived past the 4th year attained maturity status and had more chances of evading the failure (Cronin-Gilmore, 2012; Nadim & Lussier, 2010).

Researchers who analyzed the theory of management emphasized the overwhelming role played by leadership expertise when endeavoring to prevent failure (Gaskill et al., 1993). Gaskill et al. (1993) indicated that lack of management skills and expertise frequently contributed to the failure. Other studies were used to show that the business surrounding affected the factors that impacted small business enterprises (Nadim & Lussier, 2010; Walls et al., 2011). Furthermore, Beaver (2003) argued that change over a given duration altered what the small businesses required to succeed. Success depended on organization's capabilities to adapt to business environmental changes (Kamisan & King, 2013; Walls et al., 2011).

The inability of leaders to adapt to organizational changes was used to reinforce the argument that preventing small business failure depends on the leaders' competencies in managing change responsibly (Gary, 2013; Gray, 1998; Edmond, 2011; Sardana & Scott-Kemmis, 2010). Moreover, researchers argued that business environment also influenced business failure from the view of the organization's ability to compete with others in the same industry (Shaoming, Stough, & Jackson, 2009). Competition among organizations within the same industry can harm their success, as the internal competition trend undermines the organizations' capabilities to sustain their competitive advantages and performances (Cronin-Gilmore, 2012; Hunter, 2011; Nadim & Lussier, 2010). Large firms' competition was a threat to small business success and sustainability (Cronin-Gilmore, 2012). Unlike in larger firms that enjoyed economies of large scale, diseconomies of large scale was one of the severest drawbacks of small businesses to sustain successful competition and performances (Cronin-Gilmore, 2012; Nadim & Lussier, 2010).

Small business location. Other causes of small business failure beyond the factors of business environment include factors associated with the organization's geographical location (Teng et al., 2011; Walls, et al., 2011). Small businesses operating in a poor physical location stand high chances of failure (Walls et al., 2011). Walls et al. argued for the importance of the small business owner's capability to select a strategic or customer-oriented location for their business. Jensen and Pompelli (2002) explored the significance of scrutinizing features of a location when endeavored to select a viable site for a small-scale agribusiness operation. In their works, Jensen and Pompelli (2002) argued that selecting a specific location for a small agribusiness was based on the potential factors that the businesses can exploit to support the survivability.

Other researchers exploring the effects of rural locations on the small enterprises argued that the physical location of business contributed significantly toward organizational success. The argument was that an organization's level of success depended on the market share of that area (Cronin-Gilmore, 2012). Cronin-Gilmore (2012) concurred with Pena's (2002) argument that the performance outcomes of the small businesses depended on the location's significant contribution. Pena (2002) did not only focus on the issues of competitiveness within an industry, but also on the market share within various geographical regions. Every variable associated with the issue of location contributed to the possibility and manner of organizational success (Pena, 2002).

Lussier and Halabi (2010) concurred with Pena's (2002) argument that location impacted significantly successful outcomes of small businesses. The researchers argued that an owner of an organization who operated a sole business in a single area recognized the location as significant for the success of the organization (Lussier & Halabi, 2010; Pena, 2002). Moreover, Lussier and Halabi (2010) asserted that operating a business in a single area made that location crucial because of the business' sole dependency for support and survival.

Although the effects of a geographical location affect the success of small businesses, organizations need to operate with caution, as the use of online evolutions has made it possible to do business from any region (Shaoming et al., 2009). The use of E-commerce and Internet websites increasingly continue to transform the business landscape and operations at a tremendous rate (Shaoming et al., 2009). Online and the Internet capabilities influence decision-making behaviors of the modern consumers (Nadim & Lussier, 2010). Establishing online functionalities has thrown many stakeholders into a predicament concerning the continued significance of the organizational location. The Internet and online businesses often operate regardless of the features of the geographical boundaries and are likely to diminish the role of physical location in the success of small businesses (Nadim & Lussier, 2010; Shaoming et al., 2009).

Small business size. Failure of small businesses does not only result from the physical location but also the business size (Liao et al., 2009). Islam et al. (2011) explored the influences of size on businesses trying to operationally re-establish themselves after bankruptcy. Results were used to indicate that small businesses had minimal chances of rejuvenating from insolvency compared to large business organizations (Islam et al., 2011). The findings concurred with previous study findings, suggesting that small businesses possess limited resources necessary for sustainability during the unfavorable conditions (Islam et al., 2011; Wu, Song, & Zeng, 2008). Islam et al. (2011) and Wu et al. (2008) argued that small businesses were characterized with limited resources to draw from and this unique feature caused an alarming situation when adverse business circumstances happened affecting small business' success capacities. Islam et al.'s (2011) argument concurred with the assertion that owners of small businesses faced numerous threats, such as a financing quagmire in their endeavors to avoid failure (see also Arasti et al., 2012; Aterido et al., 2011).

Ellis (2012), Liao et al. (2009), and McGinn's (2004) focused on size related issues when they examined the factors that contributed to the failure of small businesses. McGinn (2004) suggested that some small business enterprises underwent an era of transformation and became too large to remain perceived as small, although they were previously too small to win the perception of being large. In the era, "no man's land," small businesses experienced a high degree of vulnerability to failure (McGinn, 2004, p. 33). Furthermore, researchers associated size when exploring the factors contributing to the failure of small businesses (Arasti et al., 2012). According to Arasti et al. (2012), small businesses failed mostly in the early stages of the organizational establishment--a time of limited size and owner's experience.

Kayemuddin (2012) offered a different view to indicate advantages of small-size to small businesses. The smaller the firm is in size, the more flexible the organization can be when managing changing technology requirements, minimizing operational costs of workforce talent development, responding quicker to meet customer demands, and identifying prime target markets (Kayemuddin, 2012; Power & Reid, 2005). Kayemuddin (2012) argued that using the conventional wisdom that bigger was better did not always indicate better outcomes in the context of leaders' large organizational departments. In contrast, the scholars advocated the significance of small businesses exploiting the advantages of their small size to enhance chances of organizational achievements (Kayemuddin, 2012).

Planning. The role of planning is central when exploring issues related to the failure of small businesses (Kantabutra, 2009). Small businesses can be successful and avoid failure through proper planning (Kantabutra, 2009; Schehr, 2011). Proper planning is a prerequisite for organizations to enhance their success chances (Kantabutra, 2009). Regardless of the leaders' expertise and business knowledge, inability to plan properly will inevitably result in failure (Kantabutra, 2009).
'

Arasti et al. (2012) conducted an in-depth exploration of the aspect of planning and small business failure. Bracker, Keats, and Pearson (1988) argued to show that businesses with unstructured planning did not succeed as the ones with structured planning. However, Lyles, Baird, Orrisis, and Kuratko (1995) suggested that no distinction existed between the structured and unstructured types of planning. Others argued that some owners of small businesses supported immensely operational planning, exhibiting limitations in strategy (Kantabutra, 2009). Small business owners need to stress unique planning approaches to small businesses to achieve the best fit (Kantabutra, 2009). Applying a planning strategy for large businesses to the small businesses inevitably results in small business failure (Kantabutra, 2009).

Culture. Beyond the factors of business size and planning, researchers used the influence of organizational culture to explain the failure of the small businesses. The culture of an organizational contributes immensely toward organizational outcomes and success (Aldrich & Martinez, 2010). Arasti et al. (2012) concurred with the works of Aldrich and Martinez (2010) who suggested the inability to comprehend differences in workforce culture could be detrimental to the success of an organization. Cultural issues influence remarkably employees' expectations or perceptions about work and consequently the manner of executing the assigned tasks (Chen, 2004; Schein, 2011).

Organizational employees with higher job satisfaction demonstrate and sustain more positive attitudes toward work when compared to employees with lower job satisfaction levels (Kamisan & King, 2013; Sosik & Cameron, 2010). Organizations with a culture of employee work satisfaction have higher employee retention rates (Kamisan & King, 2013; Sosik & Cameron, 2010). Furthermore, Schein (2011) suggested them decision about the organizational culture necessary for business success depended on the operational environment. Moreover, scholars used studies to show the significance of using organizational flexibility as a requirement in approaching problems associated with culture (Kantabutra, 2009; Sosik & Cameron, 2010).

Beyond the organization's business operation, is the existence of a culture associated with a particular business location (Walls et al., 2011). The exponents of various theories implied that a leader who had knowledge about different situations and ability to apply proper leadership practices and behaviors was likely to manage differences in cultures (Hersey

& Blanchard, 1969; Kantabutra, 2009; Rietsema & Watkins, 2012) effectively. Hersey and Blanchard (1969) advocated for the theory of strategic contingencies to stress on the leaders' behaviors based on specific situations and needs.

Darling and Leffel (2010) referred to the Boulder's general systems theory to argue that effective workforce relationships were needed to promote teamwork cohesion and performance. Organizational leaders need to understand that building adequate relationships within the workforce relies on managing individual differences, such as the ones that exist in culture (Darling & Leffel, 2010). Differences in cultural aspects originate in diverse social beliefs, norms and ethics, history, religion, and background. The strength of effective managers relies on their ability to understand the whole aspects of diversity (Morgan, 1989).

Small business leadership. Authors of various studies associated the causes of organizational failure to ineffective leadership including the leaders' inabilities to execute tasks such as researching for markets (Collins, 2005; Darling & Leffel, 2010; Johnson, 2014; Sosik & Cameron, 2010; Stanford, 1982). Nanjundaswamy and Swamy (2014) and Aterido et al. (2011) unanimously recognized that leaders with limited accurate information about pricing process stood a high chance of leading their business to failure. The inability of leaders to demonstrate adequate knowledge about satisfactory market prices for the industry's commodities and services may contribute to the failure of small firms or businesses (Jui-Chen & Silverthorne, 2005).

Research conducted on Bangladesh's small and to medium-size enterprises was used to establish that leadership affected significantly organizational outcomes (Kayemuddin, 2012). Schehr (2011) concurred in a study finding used to the emphasis on how leaders influenced organizational success. Various leadership interpretations weighed prominently on the understanding of the role played by transformational leadership concerning the failure of small businesses (Bass, 1990; Jui-Chen & Silverthorne, 2005; Sosik & Cameron, 2010). Visser, Coning, and Smit (2005) argued for the significance of transformational leadership in managing effectively the constantly changing business environments. Ellis (2012) and Thompson and Martin (2010) concurred that innovative strategies were vital in enhancing an organization's ability to prevent failure.

O'Regan and Ghobadian's (2004) through a study they explored the leadership approach, and performance confirmed the fundamental role of transformational leadership and organizational success. Bass (1990) and Visser et al. (2005) agreed with the findings of O'Regan and Ghobadian (2004) who stressed the organizational significance of transformational leadership. In their exploration, Visser et al. (2005) associated the characteristics of transformational leadership with small business entrepreneurs in South Africa and contributed to the literature of small business failure.

Transformational leadership. Sosik and Cameron (2010) argued that transformational leaders played a key role in inspiring followers to accomplish organizational goals (Avolio & Yammarino, 2013; Bass, 1990; Kouzes & Posner, 2012).

Bass (1990) used inspiration as one of the four features only in describing transformational leadership. Transformational leaders motivated followers toward attaining superior performances (Bass, 1990; Visser et al., 2005).

Bass (1990) and Visser et al. (2005) discussed three transformational leadership characteristics: intellectual stimulation, individual considerations, and charisma. The two original features of transformational leadership are interrelated. Both features are enhanced by a leader's ability to understand personal needs of individuals. According to Bass (1990), effective leaders demonstrated the ability to understand ways of stimulating individuals' intellectual capacity. One of the primary characteristics of transformational leaders is the ability to change followers' thinking behavior so they can approach current issues successfully using different or new strategies (Visser et al., 2005).

Kamisan and King (2013) argued that intellectual stimulation was used to accommodate individual's consideration. Transformational leaders recognize peoples' individual differences. Individuals possess unique characteristics at personal levels that necessitate various behavioral strategies to effect motivation (Bass, 1990). Transformational leaders create and sustain a sense of balance based on an individual's unique requirements, which dispels the bad feelings of own neglect and enhances employee motivation for completing tasks. The significance of analyzing the characteristics of transformational leadership is to assist in comprehending how different styles of leadership influenced the performance of small businesses (Kamisan & King, 2013).

Kempster and Parry (2014) viewed Charisma as the ability of leaders to earn total followers' trust in their leadership skills (see also Bass, 1990). The same manner leaders use inspiration to cause quality influence on the followers, so does the charisma. A leader demonstrates charismatic strengths by influencing a large number of followers based on the abilities to persuade persons to trust his or her leadership principles and ethics (Kempster & Parry, 2014; Visser et al., 2005; Wren, 1994). Sosik and Cameron (2010) argued that charismatic leaders exhibited competencies to inspire larger followers who in turn optimized their performance and ultimately impacted organizational success. However, Grinnell (2003) indicated that leaders tended to overemphasize on the positive aspect of charismatic factor alone and ignored the impacts of other leadership styles, such as autocratic and transactional in enhancing organizational performance.

Small Business Failure and Research Methodologies

According to Christensen et al. (2011), a methodology that was used to examine the occurrence of a phenomenon in detail was paramount in understanding the distinctive nature of the small businesses (see also Hunter, 2011). In the present study, a qualitative method was selected because the method would be used to offer a unique understanding of the factors that contributed to the failure of small businesses (Barkhuizen, 2008). Using a qualitative method allowed researchers to gain a broader perception of the entire problem (Barkhuizen, 2008; Christensen et al., 2011; Creswell, 2009). The application of a qualitative method in exploring a phe-

nomenon not only allowed the researcher to avoid using independent and dependent variables in isolation but also useful
in adopting a holistic strategy toward understanding the problem (Barkhuizen, 2008; Christensen et al., 2011)

Qualitative research. One of the primary characteristics of
qualitative research is the simultaneous gathering and materi-
alizing of the data (Creswell, 2007; Hoepfl, 1997). With qualitative research, neither prior knowledge exists about the
answers, nor do any preconceived ideas exist on what the so-
lution could be (Barkhuizen, 2008; Christensen et al., 2011;
Creswell, 2007). A qualitative method was used to uncover
numerous potential causes of failure of small businesses. In
qualitative studies, researchers focus on answering the why,
how, or what is behind, causing, or contributing to the occurrence of the phenomenon or problem (Alvesson & Sandberg,
2011; Yin, 1993). Continued existence of divergences or inconsistencies in the understanding of the failure of small businesses (Dasgupta & Sanyal, 2010) created a necessity for the
research to understand the distinctive lived experiences of
various owners of small businesses who played the key leadership or decision-making roles.

The qualitative research method requires an in-depth exploration, leading to established themes or discovering the
trends that otherwise would not be apparent in the data gathered using a quantitative method (Creswell, 2005; Farber,
2006; Gilmore, Carson, & O'Donnell, 2004; Moustakas,
1994). Similarly, Gentry (2006) argued that examining the
unique viewpoints of individuals was the focus of qualitative
research; the goal was to uncover shared meaning. Although

the qualitative method of inquiry lacks a means of establishing statistically supported causal relations among variables, the method of inquiry allowed for an in-depth understanding of relationships established in the quantitative study (Creswell, 2007).

Nevertheless, researchers universally recognized two impending faults of qualitative research. First was the potential flaw of vulnerability that resulted from the biases of the researcher (Creswell, 2007). The perceptions of the researcher can potentially direct or influence the qualitative methodology. Second was the flaw of the potential limitation related to generalizing the research findings to larger populations (Barkhuizen, 2008; Christensen et al., 2011). Qualitative methodologies involve researchers making generalizations of gained research information without proper support (Creswell, 2007). The fault results in questions about the significance of the research results. Moreover, the generalizations might constitute researcher's opinions that lack proper support (Barkhuizen, 2008; Christensen et al., 2011).

A quantitative study was considered for the current research. However, quantitative study procedures involve either rejecting or accepting of the hypotheses and therefore the data conclusions made are based on analyzed statistics (Creswell, 2007). Statistical data analysis is applied in quantitative research during endeavors to identify the causal relations between variables (Cooper & Schindler, 2003). Researchers of existing studies employed the methodologies of quantitative research and provided divergent rationales for the causes of failure of the small businesses (Barkhuizen, 2008; Christensen et al., 2011). Nevertheless, given that researchers have been unable to identify an absolute cause when employing quantitative methodologies (Creswell, 2007); there existed a need to seek for a broader and more in-depth understanding of the distinctive causes of failure of the small businesses.

Researchers who used quantitative methodologies, like in qualitative methodologies experienced certain limitations. There was the interpretation difficulty when researchers used quantitative methodologies (Creswell, 2007; Willis, 2007). Quantitative methodologies lacked adequate description or explanation of the analyzed data or statistics (Cooper & Schindler, 2003). Researchers who employed quantitative methodologies endeavored to present the statistical data in a condensed or summarized way to offer a greater understanding of the larger perspective (Neuman, 2003). Compared to other methodologies, researchers employed quantitative methodologies were challenged to determine the reasons for drawing specific conclusions (Neuman, 2003).

A mixed method research methodology was also considered for the current study. Investigating failure of small businesses, Rogoff et al. (2004) conducted a mixed method study that included features of both qualitative and quantitative methods. Mixed method research allowed for an in-depth understanding of the problem because of the partially included strategy of qualitative research (Creswell, 2007). The concept of partial was used here to mean the application of both qualitative and quantitative methods, design, and analysis in a mixed research method (Willis, 2007).

Employing a mixed research method can diminish the faults faced when using the research methodologies of quantitative and qualitative in isolation (Creswell, 2007; Willis, 2007). The flaws found in each of the quantitative and qualitative research methodologies when applied in isolation were minimized when both methodologies were used together in mixed a method (Creswell, 2007; Willis, 2007). The difficulty associated with employing a mixed research method resulted in the need to balance and pay attention evenly to both methods of research. Incorporating the quantitative research method will weaken the capacity to conduct a sole in-depth exploration of the phenomenon of failure of small businesses, which will dilute or defeat the purpose of the current study.

Qualitative research revisited. Given the advantages and disadvantages of employing the three methodologies (qualitative, quantitative, and mixed), identifying ways to minimize the shortcomings of qualitative research was critical to the current study. Identified in prior discussions was the researcher's potential to introduce bias in qualitative research (Creswell, 2007; Willis, 2007). The bias drawback intensifies when a researcher interjects personal opinions when conducting interviews and collecting data, which results in altering the reliability and validity of data gathered (Creswell, 2007).

In the study, multiple sources of data are used to minimize the flaws by countering the researcher's bias (Yin, 1993). Yin (1993) referred to the process of using multiple data sources as triangulation and emphasized triangulation's significance within a qualitative study. The present study involved examining the failure of small businesses using current literature, archival materials (such as files and books), and data gathered through interviews to increase the reliability of the data collected (Willis, 2007). It was therefore of necessity for researchers employing the qualitative method to triangulate the data from multiple sources (Creswell, 2007).

Small Business Failure and Research Design

A phenomenological design, using the van Kaam modified approach, was used to obtain a greater understanding of the studied phenomenon (Moustakas, 1994). Moustakas (1994) conversed about different qualitative approaches, such as grounded theory and ethnography. Researchers using ethnographic inquiry gain a cultural explanation through extensive group engagement and examination over an extended period (Moustakas, 1994; Van Manen, Dabbs, & Faulkner, 1982). Based on the in-depth cultural description provided in the ethnographic method of inquiry, the design was unsuitable for the purpose of the current study.

Ethnographic inquiries required the researcher to become involved in the social actions of a particular group to attain a greater understanding of the research participants investigated (Lee, 2006; Moustakas, 1994). The condition does not only fail to serve the purpose of offering an in-depth understanding of the phenomenon of failure of small business, but also pose difficulties when predicting the occurrence of a phenomenon, such as failure, or even when it could occur. A study using the grounded theory design has similar features as the ethnographic design of relying on observing and examining a group's experiences (Glaser & Strauss, 1967; Moustakas,

1994). Observing an individual, as required by a study using the ground theory design, made the design unsuitable as observing participants would not serve the purpose of the current study (Moustakas, 1994). The intrinsic phenomenological design was chosen as the best option to fulfill or serve the purpose of a study designed to explore individuals' experiences of a phenomenon using the lived experiences (Creswell, 2007; Moustakas, 1994; Willis, 2007; Ziegler, Paulus, & Woodside, 2006).

In obtaining knowledge, the current study included collecting and analyzing transcript data gathered through semi-structured interviews. Personal interviews were used in the current study to gather the information instead of observing the research participants (Creswell, 2002). Concurring with the fact, Creswell (2007) argued that interviews allowed the researcher to collect useful information when it might be difficult to observe the research participants. The type of interview to use relies on a variety of factors (Cooper & Schindler, 2003; Creswell, 2007; Willis, 2007).

Gaps in the Research Literature

Researchers of the existing studies on the failure of small business did not identify the principal cause for the increased failure rates of small businesses (Maes, Sels, & Roodhooft, 2005; Rogoff et al., 2004). Instead, the researchers advanced numerous factors that contributed to the failure of small businesses (Beaver, 2003; Stanford, 1982). Based on the divergent views about the factors that contributed to the failure, one may question or doubt the existence of the relationship between a specific factor and alarming failure rates of small businesses. In agreement with the view, Bouchikhi (1993) asserted there existed limited information about the failure of small businesses. The inability to provide a principal cause to use in enhancing the understanding of the failure of small businesses resulted in adverse effects on the societies and the understanding of theories of management (Amel & Akkari, 2012).

A review of prior research was used to reveal that the invaluable place or contribution of the small business in the U.S. economy was undeniable, as the small businesses were used to generate employment opportunities to a large portion of the local population (Schehr, 2011). Scholars argued that the significance of small businesses necessitated the need for the issue of increasing failure rates of small businesses to continue occupying a fundamental position in the thinking of organizational decision-makers and potential owners of small businesses (Temtime, Chinyoka, & Shunda, 2004).

Moreover, the unique features of small businesses required exceptional considerations (Hunter, 2011) to understand the problem. The obscurity that surrounded failure of small businesses required further research to offer a better insight concerning the predominant cause of alarming failure rates of the small businesses (Simmons, 2007). The current study will be used to add to the body of the existing knowledge about the failure of small businesses, and the stakeholders may use the knowledge to gain a better understanding of the causes of the trend of occurrence of the central phenomenon of failure of small businesses. The leaders may use the new information that will be collected concerning the happening of the phenomena primarily in the policy-making processes (Kerfoot, 2004; Kontoghiorghes & Hansen, 2004; Lipshitz & Mann, 2005; Paton, 2003).

Conclusion

The overwhelming significance of small businesses to the general U.S. economy (Cronin-Gilmore, 2012) created a need to explore small business failures to gain a greater understanding of the principal cause of the phenomenon (Amel & Akkari, 2012). The inadequacies of the existing information concerning the causes of small business failure (Bouchikhi, 1993) were used to elevate the significance of the current qualitative study to explore the phenomenon at a greater depth. A detailed examination of the present study research methodology is provided in the next chapter.

Included in the literature review was a broad historical perspective on the progression of failure of small businesses (Kline, 1974), which was the basis for understanding the factors that contributed to the failure of small businesses, such as lack of effective leadership abilities (Franco & Haase, 2010). A review of literature further used to indicate how organizational (a) location, (b) size, (c) planning, (d) culture, and (d) distinct characteristics of small businesses may contribute to the failure of small businesses. Through the literature review on the failure of small businesses, it was demonstrated that existing studies were used to emphasize on the significance of small business in driving the economy. Small business owners need to improve their leadership abilities to sustain small businesses and prevent failure of small businesses, ensure continued employment opportunities and sustain a domestic supporting economy (U.S. Census Bureau, 2014).

Summary

Included in Chapter 2 was a thorough review of literature about the causes of failure for small businesses. The chapter also encompassed various viewpoints about the occurrence of the phenomenon, presenting literature using a general to specific perspective. The literature review in Chapter 2 was used to reveal the factors contributing to the failure of small businesses including leadership and non-leadership factors such as effects of poor decisions, and organizational location, culture, size, and leadership. The inexistence of a universally accepted definition of failure resulted in researchers to use the term differently—as the term best fitted the intended purpose of the respective studies complicating an understanding of the phenomenon (Hunter, 2011). Chapter 2 also included detailed discussions on different methodologies used to explore the problem and used to focus on previous and current methodologies.

Chapter 3 is a presentation of discussion on the methodological aspects of the current study, including the research method, the research design, the guiding research question, the study population and procedures for sampling, and the procedures for obtaining informed consent and maintaining confidentiality. The appropriateness of the current study research design is also reviewed in greater depth, as it relates to the problem statement and the research purpose. Included in the chapter also is the discussion of the procedures for collecting data, the process for managing and ensuring data saturation, data collecting instrument, issues related to validity and reliability, and the data analysis process.

Chapter 3
Research Methods

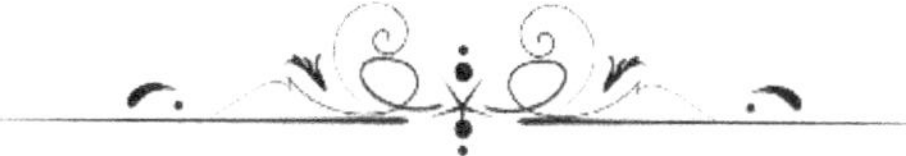

Creswell argued that researchers using open-ended questions allowed the participants to offer deeper responses while interviewing using closed-ended questions posed limitations to respondents to focus more on the theories found in the literature.

The purpose of the current qualitative phenomenological intrinsic study was to explore the lived experiences of small business owners who experienced failure of small businesses to gain an understanding of increasing failure rate trend of small businesses. According to Belinda and Allan (2014), phenomenology was the scientific study of consciousness with a focus on the intentional definition of concepts and meaning by describing the lived experiences of a shared essence (see also Creswell et al., 2007; Husserl, 1970; Scanlon, 2002; Wojnar & Swanson, 2007). The main goal of phenomenology is to understand an individual's lived experiences through hermeneutic and descriptive approaches (Belinda & Allan, 2014; Danuta & Kristen, 2007). The current study was used to focus on exploring the lived experiences of small business owners who experienced failure of small business. This may not only enhance a deeper understanding of the cause of small business failure but also how small business owners may use the knowledge to search for better options to effective decision-making strategies to sustain small businesses despite the closure.

In the current study, the researcher conducted telephone and in-depth personal interviews with a purposive sample of voluntary participants as a method of gathering the data. The participants selected for the current study possessed direct lived experiences pertaining failure of small businesses. The records of small businesses kept and maintained by the city of San Jose (2013) were used to identify and locate the participants for interviewing. Failure of small business was used in the current study refer to ceasing or closure of the business operations to avoid bankruptcy of financial losses (Ellis, 2012; Gary, 2013). Furthermore, the focus of the current study was on the phenomenon of small business failure for enterprises located in the city of San Jose, California.

Chapter 3 contains a thorough discussion of the approach to the understanding the research methodology. The sections in the chapter include the research method and design appropriateness. Also included in Chapter 3 are the research and sub-research questions and interviewing methods. Furthermore, Chapter 3 is used to cover the research population, sampling frame and data collection, confidentiality and informed consent, research instrument, and gathering of personal experiences. The conclusion of Chapter 3 includes a discussion of the issues related to validity and reliability and the description of the approach used for analyzing the interview transcripts.

Research Method and Appropriateness

The purpose of the study was to explore the lived experiences of small business owners who experienced failure to enhance understanding of the phenomenon (Creswell, 2007). According to Creswell (2007), Qualitative Research Method was used to; explore research topic, systematically design the research questions and ensure the data provided was accurate; Uncover insights, perceptions, experiences, opinions, and evaluations on lived experiences; Formulate questions of why, how, and what; Share experiences freely and build themes for analysis, and allow the researcher be the primary data collector and able to predict the outcome.

Tuleasca (2012) and Ucbasara et al. (2013) showed the predominant cause of failure of small business remained unresolved and that an in-depth assessment of the phenomenon required using a qualitative method of research. Employing a qualitative method of research allowed one to gain a broader perception of the problem examined (Creswell, 2012; Moustakas, 1996). A study involving a qualitative method required the continuous gathering of the data (Byrne, 2009; Creswell et al., 2010). There was either no prior knowledge of the answers or a preconception of what the answers could be (Creswell, 2012). With qualitative research, the study takes form and develops as the data are increasingly collected (Byrne, 2009; Creswell et al., 2010). Answers are not predetermined, and there is no existence of any predetermined idea of what the responds could be (Creswell, 2002). Therefore, the researcher determined that qualitative method was the best alternative for the current study as the method allowed exploration of numerous possibilities (Creswell, 2012) concerning the causes of small business failure.

Nevertheless, a qualitative method is associated with potential flaws. First, the methodology is susceptibility to the researchers' biases (Creswell, 2012). Second, the information obtained is useful only for generalizing the data collected (Byrne, 2009; Creswell, 2012; Creswell et al., 2010; Yin, 2009). According to Creswell (2007), the generalizations made about the information gained from qualitative research lacked support. Moreover, Creswell (2007) argued that the effect of the researcher's bias could impact significantly the results of the study. Accounting for the potential flaws identified in qualitative research, the researcher considered carefully in using either a quantitative or mixed-research research method.

Quantitative and Mixed-research. Researchers using quantitative and mixed methods rely on statistical data to draw conclusions about whether to reject or accept null hypotheses (Creswell et al., 2010). The researcher used the results based on the methodologies to analyze statistical data to identify causal relationships between variables (Creswell, 2007; "Snap Surveys Ltd.," 2009) and avoid data generalizations. However, the drawback with quantitative is that the methodologies do not offer an absolute causation (Christensen et al., 2011; Creswell, 2007; Leedy & Ormrod, 2010) that can lead to a deeper understanding of the distinct causes of failure of small businesses.

The use of the methodology of mixed methods differs slightly from the quantitative methodology (Creswell et al., 2010; "Snap Surveys Ltd.," 2009). The concern with using the methodology of mixed methods is that the researcher is compelled equally to consider both research methods—qualitative and quantitative (Creswell et al., 2010). Given the current study's purpose was to explore the lived experiences of small business owners who experienced failure of their small businesses, integrating the components of quantitative method might weaken the capacity of solely exploring the predominant cause of the phenomena at a deeper level (Creswell at el., 2010; "Snap Surveys Ltd.," 2009). The potential flaws identified with using mixed and quantitative methods led to their elimination. The qualitative method remained the best option to use ("Snap Surveys Ltd.," 2009) in the study.

Swinton-Douglas (2010) indicated much confidence in using the qualitative methodologies in various studies, implied that measures were put in place to minimize the disadvantages of a qualitative method. Yin (1993) argued that the researcher's bias during data gathering was minimized through using of multiple data sources as the process allowed data triangulation using different perspectives. Exploring the predominant cause of failure of small business using the current literature review, files from the archives, and analysis of data from the interviews was used to increase the reliability of the data gathered for the current study (Creswell et al., 2010). Triangulating data from multiple sources are therefore critical in qualitative research (Creswell, 2012; Wray, Markovic, & Manderson, 2007).

Research Design and Appropriateness

A qualitative phenomenological intrinsic design was to explore the lived experiences of the small business owners concerning failure of small businesses. According to Sokolowski (2000), phenomenological design was a descriptive approach to an inquiry. Phenomenological intrinsic design was appropriate in overcoming personal biases, as the design entailed pure personal consciousness of lived experiences (Sokolowski, 2000). Phenomenology involves not only a descriptive approach, but also a hermeneutic approach. Human beings are hermeneutic in nature because of the ability to interpret their lives and offer the meaning of the lived experiences (Moran, 2000; Van Manen, 1990). Participants would provide insight to understand the phenomenon (Pringle, Hendry, & McLafferty, 2011; Strong, Pyle, Devries, Johnston, & Foskett, 2008). Phenomenological design allowed participants to share unique the ideas, offered insights about the problem, and was best substitute for difficulties encountered in disseminating results out of quantitative method (Neuman, 2006). A qualitative phenomenological design was appropriate in answering the research questions (Neuman, 2006). In the current study, the research questions were developed after the literature review. Interviews of the research participants ensued, recording and transcribing of interviews, data organization and analysis to emerge themes.

The current study was designed using a modified van Kaam approach to gain an in-depth understanding of the occurrence or the phenomenon (Moustakas, 1996). The current study involved a structured design to gain a better understanding of the problem, which entailed elimination of the previous judgments or assumptions and concentrating in acquiring clear and bias-free findings (Blum & Muirhead, 2005; Moustakas, 1994).

The need to pursue an exploration of the fundamental distinctiveness of the phenomenon in the research reinforced the appropriateness of the phenomenological research design. Relying on the study participants' lived experiences made the phenomenological research design more suitable (Giles, 2007; Patton, 2002; Strong et al., 2008). The grounded theory design was unsuitable for the current study because researchers use grounded theory for the purpose of discovering or generating current theories (Jones & Noble, 2007).

In the current study, phenomenology was used to establish a comprehension and individual participants' interpretation of the meaning of the phenomenon, thus making an intrinsic phenomenological design more relevant (Holloway & Wheeler; 2009). Holloway and Wheeler (2009) argued that a phenomenological design allowed participants to express and describe their personal experiences (see also Moustakas, 1996; Patton, 2002). Phenomenology facilitates the gaining of a wider viewpoint about everyday practice or events (Patton, 2002; Wojnar & Swanson, 2007).

The participants' descriptions of lived experiences of failure of small businesses may lead to a better understanding of the of failure of small businesses, and small business owners leaders may use the findings to help prevent the occurrences the same phenomena. An intrinsic phenomenological design is useful for creating artifacts of the phenomenon under investigation and alleviating deficiencies associated with the current information-collecting mechanisms (Armour, Rivaux, & Bell, 2009; Patton, 2002). An intrinsic phenomenological design was used in the study because, in prior studies, scholars used the approach to acquiring information efficiently from participants who possessed distinct skills and experiences in a subject area (Creswell, 2005; Leedy & Ormrod, 2005; Patton, 2002).

Finlay (2008) advanced phenomenology in reference to the study's significance, nature and, and meaning of a phenomenon. Intrinsic phenomenological research was intended in providing thick, rich, and textured descriptions of the lived experiences; phenomenology is focused on the occurrence of events via the lived experiences (Finlay, 2008; Patton, 2002) besides the comprehension of the common phenomenon explored. The current study, therefore, was based on the intrinsic phenomenological research design (Conklin, 2007; Moustakas, 1996; Patton, 2002).

Explanatory design was considered for the current study. However, the inability of the design to provide sufficient detail describing the data was a major issue that hindered understanding the distinct nature of the happening of the phenomenon (Alvesson & Sandberg, 2011; Christensen, Johnson, & Turner, 2011; Moustakas, 1996); therefore, the design was eliminated as an alternative. Researchers argued that other types of qualitative designs would not result in achieving the intended goal of the research (Creswell, 2010), such as to gain a better understanding of small business failure. The flaws identified made the other designs unsuitable for the current study. Creswell (2010) argued that designs, such as historical narrative, content analysis, ethnographic, heuristics, case study, and Delphi inadequately led to exploring a shared phenomenon.

Typically, phenomenology involved a sample size of 10 to 25 entities who possessed direct experience of the explored phenomenon (Leedy & Ormrod, 2005). The study's represented the small business population from the south, east, and west localities of San Jose, California. Small businesses in the three developed localities represented the major contributing sectors to the micro-economy.

Interviewed was a sample of 10 small business owners who experienced failure of their small businesses representing two participants from each of the seven sectors: (a) recreational, (b) wholesale and retail, (c) service, (d) construction, (e) housing, and (f) transportation and communications. Qualitative phenomenological studies involve extensive 1 or 2-hour interviews with carefully selected participants (Leedy &

Ormrod, 2005). In the present study, the researcher used semi-structured interviews that included open-ended questions. The interview questionnaire allowed the gathering of detailed information (Bloomberg & Volpe, 2008).

The researcher in the current study utilized a phenomenological intrinsic design, using the modified Van Kaam approach to enhance the comprehension of the shared phenomenon (Moustakas, 1996; van Manen 1990). The modified van Kaam approach is used instead of other inquiries of a qualitative study, such as grounded theory and ethnography because the approach allows the researcher to focus on understanding the problem as the participants describe their lived experiences of the central phenomena (Moustakas, 1994). The goal of grounded theory and ethnographic designs is to explore individual's experiences to enhance the understanding of a phenomenon (Moustakas, 1996) but the concern with the designs is that the research is required to observe the happening of the phenomenon physically. Moreover, the inability of the researcher to predict the occurrence of the phenomenon hinders physical observation, and the flaw led to a rejection of the grounded theory and ethnographic designs.

The participants' interview responses were transcribed for analysis (Creswell, 2007; Woods, 2011). In the study, personal and telephone interviews were used for gathering the data unlike in grounded theory and ethnographic designs which require the researcher's physical observation of the phenomenon's happening. Creswell (2007) and Woods (2011) argued that personal interviews allowed researchers to gather valuable data whenever observing of the participants is difficult.

Qualitative research often involves unstructured interviewing, to allow primarily the participants opportunity to provide divergent views when answering the questions (Woods, 2011). The unstructured type of interview applied pertinently in qualitative research allows broader participant's responses different from interviews used in quantitative and mixed method research (Christensen et al., 2011; Creswell, 2012; Leedy & Ormrod, 2010; Neuman, 2006; Woods, 2011). Given the purpose of the current qualitative phenomenological intrinsic study was to explore the lived experiences of small business owners concerning the failure of small business to understand the cause of small business failure, unstructured interviewing using open-ended questions was necessary (Moustakas, 1996). Creswell (2007) argued that quantitative research interviews were structured with closed-ended questions to allow the investigator to gather relevant theoretical information found in the literature. Nevertheless, structured interviews with closed-ended questions do not allow the interviewer to gain deeper responses to questions (Christensen et al., 2011; Creswell, 2007; Leedy & Ormrod, 2010; Neuman, 2006; Woods, 2011).

Semi-structured interviews included both closed and open-ended questions (Creswell, 2007). Woods (2011) concurred with Creswell's (2007) view that interviews using open-ended questions solely led to the only partial understanding of the problem. Furthermore, using closed-questions solely as in structured interviews limits the participant's responses. Researchers use closed-ended questions in mixed and quantitative research methods more strictly than in qualitative research (Christensen et al., 2011; Creswell, 2007; Leedy & Ormrod, 2010; Neuman, 2006; Woods, 2011).

After examining the advantages and disadvantages of every type of interview, the researcher determined that semi-structured interviews using both open and closed-ended questions were the most suitable approach to meeting the purpose of the current study (see Appendix A). It is essential to gather information to use in enhancing an understanding of the relationship between the information collected through crossed-ended questioning and theories of small business leadership behavior. The advantage of the semi-structured interview is that the researcher capitalizes on using both closed and open-ended questions. Creswell (2012) argued that researchers using open-ended questions allowed the participants to offer deeper responses while interviewing using closed-ended questions posed limitations to respondents to focus more on the theories found in the literature. An in-depth understanding of previous theories in the literature exploring small business owner's decision-making practices effects may be attained through closed-ended questioning (Creswell, 2012).

Creswell (2012) and Neuman (2006) argued that pairing open and closed-ended questions wherever required allowed the participant to expand further on answers to closed-ended questions. When participants are asked to offer personal perceptions of the small business owner's decision-making practice contributing to the failure of the small business, it may require the pairing of open and closed interview questions. Although utilized to enhance the understanding of small business failure, closed-ended questions limited participants' responses when discussing how lived experiences affected the perception (Creswell, 2012; Woods, 2011). In such a situation, open-ended follow-up questions allow individuals to provide a deeper understanding of responses, using personal lived experiences to support their responses.

Research and Sub-Research Questions

The goal of the current study was to understand the phenomenon of failure of small businesses by exploring the lived experiences of small business owners who have experienced failure of their small business. A review of several studies was used to reveal continued inability to prevent consistent failure rates of small businesses (U.S. Department of Commerce, 2013; U.S. Small Business Administration, 2011), implying a misunderstanding existed about the predominant cause for the failure of small businesses. Moreover, a review of the literature did not reveal any research exploring the inconsistencies.

The focus of the research question for the current study was on discovering the predominant causes of failure of small businesses. The central RQ used in guiding the current study was, ; how do small business owners who experienced failure perceive and interpret the meaning of the lived experiences? The research question was used to elicit an honest and reliable description of direct lived experiences of small owners who experienced failure of their small businesses (Swinton-Douglas, 2010). The focus of the central research question was on eliciting business leaders' firsthand experiences of failure of small business. The study's goal was not to entail identifying relationships among variables or on examining trends, rather examining a central phenomenon. The goal was to gain a better understanding of how small business owners perceive and describe their experiences concerning the central phenomenon of small business failure (Bloomberg & Volpe, 2008; Neuman, 2005). Performing qualitative research, researchers used participants and sites to understand a central phenomenon (Creswell, 2005).

The following research sub-questions were used to support the main research question:

- What is the perception and interpretation of small business owners who experienced failure about the unique features of small businesses contributing to the failure of small businesses?
- What is the perception and interpretation of small business owners who experienced failure about leadership causing failure of small businesses?
- How do small business owners who experienced failure perceive and interpret non-leadership factors, such as business location, and size contributing to the failure of small businesses?

The first sub-research question was used to focus on the perception of the unique features representing common elements of the business entity that could lead to failure. Small business owners function as policy makers of their small businesses and contribute to ensuring the success of small business and discovering new opportunities (Islam, Khan, Obaidullah, & Alam, 2011). Small business owners play a vital role in success or failure of small businesses, as the process of effective entrepreneurship is about providing or enhancing leadership competencies to manage complex business tasks and issues (Islam et al., 2011). Berte et al. (2010) argued that owners of small businesses operated the businesses characterized by limited resources. The unique feature limits the activities of small businesses such as formulating the core strategic business capabilities necessary for successful competition, which results in failure.

The focus of the second sub-research question was on the perceptions of specific leadership abilities that contributed to the failure of small businesses. Small business owners play the leadership role by acting as the decision-makers; they formulate and develop the business' strategic plans, initiate and establish strategic competition to achieve the business' goals, and improve the strategies that result in marginal revenue from investments (Emale, 2010). The small business owners' decision-making practices affect the business' marketing, operational, and financial strategies, despite failure. Small business owners who demonstrate effective leadership styles enhance the efficiency of small business operations may help in preventing failure (DeCaro et al., 2010). Small business owners who lack efficient organizational leadership styles contribute to the failure of their businesses (Çakar & Ertürk, 2010).

The focus of the third sub-research question was on the perception of non-leadership related causes that may contribute to the failure of small businesses. The potential causes included organizational location, size, funding, culture, and learning. The ability of leaders to adjust successfully to the dynamic business environment may prevent failure of small businesses (Fard et al., 2009).

Interviews.

Supported by the sub-research questions, the research question was used to guide the study's investigation. Open-ended interview questions were used to avoid limiting the responses of the participants (Creswell, 2012). The framing of the questions aligned appropriately with semi-structured and unstructured interview requirements (Creswell et al., 2010). Interviews using open-ended questions do not limit the participants in their responses, rather used to offer a frame of reference for answering the questions (Woods, 2011).

Personal interviews are used to provide an opportunity to the interviewer using semi-structured and unstructured interviewing to examine individuals' experiences (Moustakas, 1996; Swinton-Douglas, 2010). Given the purpose of the qualitative phenomenological intrinsic study was to explore the lived experiences of small business owners who have experienced failure of their small business, the research question was preliminary to allow the researcher gain a deeper understanding of the problem (Swinton-Douglas. 2010). Similar to in-depth interviews, the goal of using interview questions (see Appendix A) was to encourage the participants in sharing of relevant data and information (Creswell, 2012; Swinton-Douglas, 2010).

Various reasons existed for gathering data using personal and telephone interviews instead of email or focus groups. Interviews using focus groups were eliminated because of the uncertainty associated with the interaction abilities of the target group. Using focus group interviews results in effective outcomes only when the participants can interact and cooperate among themselves (Creswell, 2010). The homogeneous sample used by the researcher in focus group interviews would pose concern of not being able to predict the number of the owners of small businesses who failed and are willing to participate in the research. Anticipated difficulties in determining the participants' interaction before the meeting led to eliminating the focus group interview type.

Creswell (2010) argued that interviews using email were the third alternative whenever personal, and telephone interviews fail. Creswell (2010) asserted that using email addresses could allow the researcher access to a broader population. Emails were used as a tool to follow up the interview discussion. If personal and telephone interviews were scheduled successfully, then there could be no need to make plans for email interviewing.

The current study did not involve professional interviewers. The researcher conducted interviews by the required guidelines to maximize participation and willingness to share information (Creswell, 2012; Neuman, 2006; Woods, 2011). The researcher monitored the whole interview process from the genesis to the conclusion (Creswell, 2012; Neuman, 2006; Woods, 2011). The interviewer followed the recommended techniques for probing, establishing rapport, and generating an enjoyable experience for the participants (Creswell, 2010; Woods, 2011). The current study involved digital recording and transcribing of every interview for quality and improvement reporting of the lived experiences of small business owners who experienced failure of their small businesses. The researcher expressed appreciation to the participants and make copies of all notes and transcripts upon completing the interviews.

Population, Sampling Frame, Data Collection

The focus of the existing research examining the issue of failure of small businesses was on particular features of the small businesses. According to U.S. Small Business Administration (2011), the subject of failure of small business was discussed from the perspective of borrowers and the recipients of the guaranteed loans (Edmister, 1972). Edmister (1972) argued that a researcher could apply such categorization to narrow the focus and increase the insight of the relationships between the ratios of finance and forecasting failure. Gaskill et al. (1993) explored Iowa retail stores with the specific interest in the causes of closure for accessory and apparel stores. The current study was used to follow similar causes of the stores' closure. The population was limited to small businesses in San Jose, California, but not to a specific industry.

Population. The current study's population comprised of San Jose, small business owners who experienced a business failure within five years of opening operations. The sample consisted of San Jose small business owners who directly experienced failure and are willing to participate voluntarily in the study. The public records the city of San Jose maintains were used to identify and locate small business owners for interview participation.

The researcher utilized the current listing directory stored and maintained by the city of San Jose, California. The sample characteristics remained unknown because of inability to predict which of the small business owners were willing to participate in the current study. Creswell (2012) argued that the approach used in the sampling affected the selection of available sites or individuals.

Sampling Frame. A typical sample size for a study with a phenomenological design is up to 20 participants (Rudestam & Newton, 2007). Compared to quantitative studies, qualitative studies often have a smaller sample size (Walker, 2007). Studies involving phenomenological design may have a sample size of one individual or a group of eight to 12 individuals participating in thorough interviews to share their personal experiences (Walker, 2007). In the current study, purposive sampling was used to select the participants because each participant must have possessed knowledge about the phenomenon of failure of a small business (Creswell, 2005; Creswell & Plano Clark, 2007; Haverkamp & Young, 2007). The participants were small business owners who either had direct experiences of failure of small business and whose business had no more than 100 employees. The researcher continued with sampling until data saturation is attained.

Ten participants were interviewed using semi-structured questions to increase understanding of the phenomenon of small business failure. The point of saturation was attained after Participant 8 was interviewed as Participants 9, and 10 did not yield any new information. Moreover, Creswell (2002) argued that in qualitative research, examining a limited number of sites or individuals increased the understanding of a problem and that examining of an extra participant decreased the problem's depth of understanding (Creswell, 2002).

Telephone interviews of purposively selected participants were conducted to collect the data. A homogeneous type of sampling was used, allowing the researcher to sample select sites or people based on a distinct location or specific group characteristics (Creswell, 2012). Random samples in qualitative research are attained through purposive sites or individual selection used to enhance an understanding the explored phenomenon (Creswell, 2012). The sample included small business owners with the personal experience of small business failure willing to participate voluntarily in the current study. Participants were purposely selected for the current study based on five criteria: (a) the number of employees in the small business must not have exceeded 100; (b) independently owned and operated; (c) the small business could not be a key player in the industry (USSBA, 2011); (d) the business must have located in San Jose, California; and (e) the current contact information for the small business owners must be available. Following Creswell's (2010) advice, the researcher used distinct characteristics purposefully to recognize information rich small business owners from the directory kept and maintained by officials from the city of San Jose, California. The participants' selection was based on the following unique five characteristics: (a) the owners of the small businesses had less than 100 workers, (b) the owners of small business owned the small business independently, (c) the small business was not a key player in that industry or sector (U.S. Small Business Administration, 2005), (d) San Jose localities must have been the geographical location for the small business the small business, and (e) the owner of small business must exist with the most current contacts. Information rich small business owners enhanced the researcher's understanding of the phenomenon. To reduce the potential bias, the participant selection was based on the order of their responses. Identifying small business owners who failed provided information rich (Creswell, 2002) knowledge to enhance the researcher's insight of failure of small businesses. The information rich selection was also used to increase insight about the relationship between failure of small business and location because the information rich small business owners could provide distinct views about the phenomenon.

Selected sites for interviewing did not depend on a particular requirement concerning failure of small businesses. A geographical location selected was convenient for the participants, central, inexpensive and safe. The site was to be easy to monitor the research process and ensure protocol compliance during data collection from the participants (Creswell, 2010).

The coding of the transcripts allowed the development of themes and easier to recognize the emerging themes from the next interviews. The interviews continued until the point of sample saturation was achieved--when no new themes emerge. Exploring a limited number of sites or individuals was used increase an understanding of the problem (Creswell, 2010). Creswell (2010) argued that in qualitative research, the depth of the problem insight may diminish with when new participants are added to the study (Creswell, 2010).

Confidentiality

The requirement of conducting personal and telephone interviews with small business owners necessitated that the participants complete waivers before participating in interviews. Cooper and Schindler (2003) argued that a waiver could include four pieces of information: (a) that participants have a right to refuse to answer the questions, (b) the time required to participate in the research, (c) a section for participant's written permission of inclusion, and (d) information regarding the privacy of the data collected. The participants needed to be assured of the measures that would be taken to guarantee the protection of the information gathered and that a written consent was required before their information is made public.

Even if the current study's results are published, the participants needed to be informed that their names and individual data would remain confidential. The sensitive data and names gathered were to be coded to ensure participant confidentiality (Creswell, 2012; Woods, 2011). In the current study, the names of the participants were to be replaced with the word interviewee and the matching numbers allocated for the interview, unless the participant decides to publish his or her name through written permission.

Informed Consent

A statement sent to the participant for signature before participating in research was called an informed consent form (Neuman, 2005). The content of the informed consent form was used to inform the participants of certain rights guaranteed if they decided to participate (Bloomberg & Volpe, 2008; Creswell, 2005; Neuman, 2005). Following the guidance of Neuman (2005), every interview was to be scheduled or performed only with the participant's acknowledgment by signing the letter of informed consent (see Appendix B). The researcher provided the interview schedule with date, phone list, and times.

The letter of consent details the rights of the participant, in the case of withdrawal from the current study at any time (Neuman, 2005). The letter also was used to explain the potential danger or benefits of participating in the research. In the case of withdrawal, the researcher would email a statement to confirm the participant's withdrawal before commencing of the interview. Withdrawing during interviews would necessitate the researcher to terminate the interview and cancel all documents already filled and signed. To withdraw after the interview, the participant would email the researcher within three days after completing the interview, and the researcher ensured immediate destruction of all documents, including both soft and hard copies. The researcher informed the participant of the non-inclusion of the gathered data in the current study (Bloomberg & Volpe, 2008; Creswell, 2005; Neuman, 2005).

In the current study, properly managing data involved a system of tracking and complete filing (Johns Hopkins University, 2008). The study also involved separating and properly coding the letters of informed consent, the transcripts from the interviews, and participants' private information for confidentiality reasons. The researcher provided every participant with a code number and a single digital master list document that linked the code numbers to the respective participants. A password protected computer hard drive was used to store safely the digital master list at the researcher's residence for seven years after dissertation completion before the entire information destroyed.

Once the University of Phoenix Institutional Review Board provided approval for the research project, the following steps occurred with potential participants. The first step was a letter mailed to potential participants requesting participation in the research (see Appendix C). The second step entailed mailing the informed consent form (see Appendix B), requesting that participant's sign, seal, and return the consent form in the provided stamped envelope. The third step involved mailing participants a letter of appreciation thanking them for agreeing to participate in the research (see Appendix D), specifying when the researcher called to schedule a one-one interview.

Geographic Location

San Jose, California was the location of the population for the small business owners to participate in the current study. However, the geographical location would vary within San

Jose depending on the area the small business owners operated the businesses. The researcher recognized the information rich participant area (Creswell, 2010) in the south, north, east, and west regions of San Jose for easy identification of the participants.

The order of response from the potential participants and properly filled out forms of consent received were used to determine the selection of participants. A mutually convenient place and time were scheduled to conduct each one-on-one interview, and if a personal interview were not feasible, a telephone interview would be scheduled. The majority of participants completed the informed consent form at the interview site to guarantee a physical copy. The researcher provided the option of accepting a facsimile copy of consent form in case of a telephone interview.

Instrumentation

A qualitative phenomenological intrinsic study requires instrumentation as the measuring tools. Researchers use research questions to align to the method of data collection and analysis (Leedy & Ormrod, 2010). The study involved a one-on-one, written and telephone interviewing of small business owners who experienced failure to achieve optimal rigor and credibility of the study.

The study involved 16 semi-structured interview questions (see Appendix A) designed to enhance lived expressions of the participants that would result in an in-depth understanding of the phenomena (Colaizzi, 1978). Participants of the field test for the study constituted of three scholars in business management - organizational leadership who were asked to form a panel of experts to help in establishing the face reliability and validity of the interview questions for easy reading and understanding (Creswell, 2006). Creswell (2006) argued that field testing of interview questions by a panel of experts was used to modify interview questions when necessary.

In the study, three experts in business management entrepreneurship field tested the interview questions of the proposal before submission and made two recommendations of the interview questions. One, the interview questions needed expansion from the limited number of five to a number that would allow the gathering of data sufficient for the study. Second, the interview questions needed rewording for clarity and consistency. The field testing of interview questions resulted in the reframing of the interview questions and extension from five to 16 interview questions.

The software NVivo10® tool was used for the current qualitative study because researchers use the software to identify emerging themes from the data collected during interviews (Creswell, 2002; Johns Hopkins University, 2008; Neuman, 2003). The researcher conducted semi-structured interviews to provide information supporting present theories in the discipline and offering unique information based on the interviewees' experiences (Creswell, 2012; Neuman, 2006; Pringle et al., 2011).

The next step was the recording of the entire interview, ensuring the transcription and verification of recordings were completed and entering information into the Microsoft Word® for accuracy and clarity. The data were subsequently imported into NVivo10 for analysis. Verbal consent was obtained to record all phone interview conversations. The researcher transcribed the telephone interview notes, validated with phone conversations recording, type using Microsoft Word version for clarifications and accuracy, and was imported to NVivo 10 for analysis.

The instrument of semi-structured questions involved in the present qualitative study allowed more flexibility of the research interviews than is the case in a quantitative study that involves structured interviews (Cohen & Crabtree, 2006). The more flexibility of semi-structured interviews in the current study was used to generate a framework that is reasonably open and flexible (Woods, 2011). The sections into which the interview questions of the study fell included: unique characteristics of small businesses, leadership, non-leadership factors such as small business location, planning, size, and culture. Each of the broad section contained questions on the failure of small businesses.

The legitimacy of a study depends on its reliability and validity. Researchers take necessary actions to ensure legitimacy establishment. Reliability of a qualitative study is equated to dependability, validity is to credibility, and generalizability is viewed as transferability (Bloomberg & Volpe, 2008). The purpose of the pilot study and instrument face-validation was to enhance reliability and validity.

Gathering of Personal Experiences

The selection of personal and telephone interviews to use in gathering personal information about lived experiences is influenced by many factors. Officials of the city of San Jose maintain updated listings of small business owners that the researcher used to contact potential participants quickly and conveniently schedule a larger population for personal interviews. City officials allow the public access to the current directory listings without any permission, requirements, or restrictions.

Interviews by telephone were a secondary alternative for initial or follow-up interviews in the absence of a personal meeting. Conducting interviews by telephone were the second alternative because of its shortcomings. When conducting telephone interviews, researchers often have difficulties obtaining sufficient and accurate information (Pringle et al., 2011). Furthermore, telephone interviewing yields lower rates of response compared to other interview techniques (Pringle et al., 2011; Woods, 2011). Pringle et al. (2011) indicated that it might become difficult for the researcher to contact many targeted individuals in cases where phone number listings were not current.

The problem may be avoided in a homogeneous sampling study because of the sampling convenience, which involves purposefully selecting individuals for interviews. Purposeful selection allows the interviewer to pick a sample from the population using the updated phone directory of small business owners. Furthermore, Creswell (2012) compared homogeneous sampling to convenience sampling based on the availability and willingness of study participants to be examined. The increased rate of responses improved the analysis of the phenomena or problem that was the failure of small business.

The second advantage of telephone and personal interviews was they allowed the researcher to control unforeseen data gathering occurrences (Creswell, 2010; Neuman, 2006). For example, when asking participants questions about their lived experiences, some answers may require further clarification. The interviewer may also face challenging moments due to an uncertainty of responses about individual experiences that may require added information.

In situations that require clarification of information, the researcher would contact the participants and schedule a follow-up interview for one week after the initial interview. The follow-up interviews would involve telephone interviews to gain a deeper understanding of the interviewees' responses. Researchers find interviews by telephone to be cost and time effective (Creswell, 2012; Neuman, 2006; Woods, 2011).

Reliability and Validity

Qualitative researchers use authenticity, dependability, confirmability, truthfulness, transferability and credibility same way reliability and validity are used commonly in quantitative research (Lincoln & Guba, 1985). Lincoln and Guba (1985) argued that trustworthiness was significant in attaining reliability. Trust was key in the study that involved 10 small business owners who experienced failure in a particular geographical location, pilot participants each subjected to meeting the research parameters. The worthiness of the research depended on the relevant evaluation of the study (Lincoln & Guba, 1985).

Credibility was used to refer to the truthful confidence of research findings and transferability meant the applicability of the research findings in various contexts (Lincoln & Guba, 1985). Conformability was the manner the findings were constructed from the participants point of view and not the research (bias-free findings) (Lincoln & Guba, 1985). While dependability was used for the consistency of the findings and the researcher did not expect to generalize the same findings in every similar setting (Bloomberg & Volpe, 2008). Truthfulness enhances the legitimacy and reliability of the study (Creswell, 2005).

According to Pringle et al. (2011), researchers could minimize the threats that might affect the capability to make accurate conclusions about collected data. Although Newman (2006) argued that it was difficult to attain perfect reliability and validity, this view could not be used as an excuse to ignore specific issues of concern in research or studies that may impact reliability and validity. Part of validity in a qualitative study is the field testing of the interview questions and the results to ensure that the researcher captures the required data (Newman, 2006). The researcher's goal is to ensure the reliability of the measures used (Creswell, 2010). In turn, the reliability of an instrument or measure used influences the validity of the generated data (Creswell, 2010).

The participant selection process may potentially threaten the internal validity of research because the characteristics of the chosen individuals for a study may represent threats that can affect the outcome's accuracy. Such threats include selecting participants who are unwilling to respond honestly to the questions (Creswell, 2012). Creswell

(2012) argued that randomly selecting participants could help minimize internal validity threats. In the study, the participants were selected purposefully relying on distinct characteristics for identifying information-rich participants to ensure accurate study findings. Furthermore, triangulating the data sources would be used to support validity and reliability of the findings.

Pringle et al. (2011) argued that validity was the researcher's ability to make reliable inferences about data. However, external validity threats inhibit the researcher's ability to make accurate generalizations of the results relating to other populations. The current study's external validity depended on the extent to which the results applied to the owners of other small businesses.

The current study's population was small business owners who experienced failure of small businesses located in San Jose, California. The selected participants represented information rich (Creswell, 2010) sources who would contribute to a deeper understanding of the phenomenon and help in acceptance of data generalizations. The researcher also minimized the threats to external validity through endeavors to make the research participation convenient for information rich (Creswell, 2010) owners of small business owners.

The interviews were scheduled at convenient locations for individual participants. The described selection procedure of owners of small business was used to generalize the findings to other owners of small businesses only in same geographical location. The generalization may not apply to small business owners located in other cities as small businesses in various cities may be are uniquely characterized. There were no generalizations made without data corroboration from similar research in various national regions.

Pilot Study.

In the research, a pilot study was conducted for the purpose of validating the reliability of the interview process. Five small business owners who experienced failure of the small businesses from the population were requested to participate in the pilot study after the IRB approval. The pilot study participants validated the reliability of interview questions prior conducting main interviewing of the 10 selected research participants. Records maintained by the city of San Jose were the source of the five pilot study participants.

The participants of the pilot study recommended minor modifications of the interview questions. Interview questions were insignificantly reworded for clarity enhancement and allowed the participants' direct address to the questions (Neuman, 2006). The validity and appropriateness of the interview questions were confirmed though the information was not included in data analysis of the study (Neuman, 2006).

A pilot study is a mini version of a complete study used for pre-testing of particular instruments to be used such as interview questions or questionnaires (Van Teijlingen & Hundley, 2001). Van Teijlingen and Hundley (2001) argued that the perception of the pilot study as an outstanding research design did not automatically ensure a general success of the entire study. The pilot study was useful in obtaining prior notice especially when the main inquiry was likely to fail, the research protocols not likely to be followed, or when the instruments suggested were likely unsuitable for the research (Van Teijlingen & Hundley, 2001).

Analysis of Personal Experiences

The analysis of the personal experiences collected would require extensive use of qualitative research tools. NVivo10 software was used for the qualitative data collected, and Microsoft Word was the repository for the qualitative research information collected. The analysis of the qualitative research information followed a procedural strategy.

Data-reporting process entailed a systematic review of transcripts, identification of relevant units, textural-structural description, and individual textural descriptions. The Software was used to label, organize, and code relevant data that emerged from the participants' responses (Neuman, 2006).

The interviewer created a coding system for easy analysis of data after entry into the Microsoft Word. Initially, the entry coding system was guided using themes, focusing on areas including the causal perceptions of failure; descriptions of cons and pros of lived experiences of small business owner's decision making practices effects on employee satisfaction and retention, motivation and encouragement, team and group building, coaching, training and learning, performance evaluation and feedback, marketing, operations, and finances leading to failure; and demographic information. The researcher tracked the system of coding in a book as a way of reference concerning the building up of different categories of data. The coding system functioned as a guide to ensure accurate transferring of data into NVivo10.

The researcher used the NVivo10 software, clustering the information by themes, and the consecutive approximation assisted in understanding the individual's lived experiences. Newman (2006) argued that consecutive approximation enhanced the clarification of issues because new knowledge was acquired whenever the issues were revisited. Successive or repeatedly revisiting the problem allowed the researcher to move away from vague understanding toward a comprehensive understanding (Neuman, 2006). The researcher of a study uses a methodology that allows for generalizations depending on a comprehensive analysis.

Summary

The qualitative methodology was used to enhance the understanding of the central phenomenon of failure of the small businesses. Creswell (2010) argued that qualitative methodologies offered individuals a distinctive way of gaining insights of the problem studied. In the current study, the instruments of personal and telephone interviews played the primary role in gaining the insight.

The researcher gained a unique perspective about the problem of the failure of small business by interviewing small business owners. Chapter 4 includes a description of the results of the phenomenological study. Included in Chapter 4 is a detailed description of the data collections and analysis. The data findings and reports are also provided to explain the experiences of the participants.

Chapter 4
Results

■ Ten participants were interviewed using semi-structured questions to enhance understanding of the phenomenon of small business failure. Personal interviews with participants were conducted to collect the data. A homogeneous type of sampling was used, which allowed researchers to sample select sites or people based on distinct location or specific group characteristics.

The purpose of the qualitative phenomenological intrinsic study was to explore the lived experiences of small business owner leaders who experienced failure of small businesses. A qualitative phenomenological method is a strategic procedure used in conducting research examining and describing perceptions of the peoples' lived experiences (Willis, 2007). Willis (2007) argued that phenomenology, as used in behavioral sciences, allowed researchers to listen carefully to the detailed accounts of lived experiences without interruption to construct accurate scientific guesses of what happened by putting together keywords used by the participants an during interview. *The central research question (RQ) for the study, "How do owner leaders of small business who experienced failure perceive and interpret the lived experiences?"* was used to focus on discovering the predominant cause of failure of small businesses.

The techniques used to collect the data for both the pilot and the main study involved use of in-depth, open-ended interviews and observations as advocated by Creswell (2008). Researching issues of failure of small businesses were used to offer an opportunity to enhance insight into lived experiences and perceptions of 10 owner leaders of small businesses who experienced failure of small businesses as participants in in-depth, open-ended interviews. Investigating the shared lived experiences, opinions, and perceptions enhanced the understanding of causes of failure of small businesses. .

Personal and telephone interviews were performed involving small business owners who experienced failure of small businesses and voluntarily agreed to participate in the study, purposively sampled for data collection. The public records maintained by the city of San Jose, California formed the source of identifying and locating the small business owner leaders who experienced failure of small businesses for interviewing. For the purpose of the study, failure of small businesses meant termination of operations of organizational businesses to prevent further financial loss or bankruptcy (Headd, 2003). Furthermore, the study was with specific interest in the failure of small businesses located in the city of San Jose, California.

Discussion of Research Methodology

Presented in Chapter 4 is a detailed exploration of the lived experiences of 10 owner-leaders of small businesses who experienced failure , starting with the synopsis of the data collection process. The discussion about the process of data collection is focused on the van Kaam Modified approach (Moustakas, 1994) to analyze the data. Continued in Chapter 4 is the presentation of the interview (IQs) presentation, which involved the significance of the questions to the study, and each participant's response to the questions.

The research was used to allow easier investigation and identification of the participants' core perceptions concerning the failure of small businesses and possible prevention means. Explained in Chapter 4 is the data collection and analysis for the study and interview questions. Chapter 4 contains a summary of the gathered data findings as generated from in-depth, open-ended interviews with 10 participants, a sample of the study, demographic sample, and the results from the analyzed data resulting from the interviews.

Research Sampling Procedures

The population for the current qualitative phenomenological study consisted of small business owner leaders who experienced failure of the businesses. The sample consisted of small business owners who directly experienced failure and were willing to participate voluntarily in the study. The public records maintained by the city of San Jose were used to identify and locate the small business owner leaders for interview participation. The researcher utilized the current listing directory maintained by city employees of San Jose, California. The sample characteristics remained unknown because of inability to predict as to which of the small business owners could be willing to participate in the current study.

Creswell (2012) argued that a particular approach used in any sampling affected the selection of available sites or individuals. In the study, purposive sampling was used to select the participants because each participant possessed knowledge about the phenomenon (Creswell, 2005; Creswell & Plano Clark, 2007; Haverkamp & Young, 2007) of failure of a small business. The participants were small business owner leaders who directly experienced failure of small businesses and whose businesses comprised no more than 100 employees. The researcher continued with sampling until data saturation was attained.

Ten participants were interviewed using semi-structured questions to enhance understanding of the phenomenon of small business failure. Personal interviews with participants were conducted to collect the data. A homogeneous type of sampling was used, which allowed researchers to sample select sites or people based on distinct location or specific group characteristics (Creswell, 2012). Random samples in qualitative research are attained through purposive sites or individual selection used to enhance an understanding of the explored phenomenon (Creswell, 2012).

The sample included owners of small businesses who experienced failure of small businesses and were willing to participate voluntarily in the study. Participants were purposively selected for the current study based on five criteria: (a) the number of employees in the small business must not have exceeded 100; (b) the small business was independently owned and operated; (c) the small business was not a key player in the industry (USSBA, 2011); (d) the business was located in San Jose, California; and (e) the updated contact information for the small business owners was available. The criteria resulted in distinct features used in identifying information rich small business owner leaders from the listings kept and maintained by the city of San Jose. Information rich small business owner leaders enhanced the researcher's understanding of the phenomenon of failure of small businesses (Creswell, 2002).

The interview transcripts were coded to develop themes and easily recognized the emerging themes out of the interviews that followed. The interviews continued until data saturation point was attained when no new information emerged. The number of participants interviewed was limited to enhance the understanding of the problem (Creswell, 2010). Creswell (2010) argued that in qualitative research, the in-depth of the research problem insight diminished with new, more or added study participants.

The selection and participation request were through the

postal mail using the Participation Request Letter (see Appendix C). The Informed Consent and Confidentiality Form (see Appendix B) accompanied the Participation Request Letter to be signed and returned in a stamped and self-addressed envelope before conducting interviews. A letter was sent to the selected potential participants notifying of the future Interview Participation (see Appendix E).

Sample Selection and Description

One hundred and fifty letters were mailed to the potential participants explaining the purpose of the study and requesting participation that generated 12 possible participants. The next mailing of 100 letters to potential participants generated additional five possible participants for a total of 17 participants. Four possible participants declined to participate, and two returned the signed consent form late. Upon the commencement of the interview process, one of the potential participants died suddenly before interviewed, and the sample size was reduced to 10 participants. The point of saturation was attained after Participant 8 was interviewed as Participants 9, and 10 did not yield any new information. Moreover, Creswell (2002) argued that in qualitative research, examining a limited number of sites or individuals increased the understanding of a problem and that examining of a new participant decreased the problem's depth of understanding (Creswell, 2002).

Considering to represent a diverse group of individuals with information rich (Creswell, 2002), the study involved participants who operated businesses in five parts of San Jose City: east, west, south, north, and downtown San Jose, offering invaluable insights concerning the failure of small businesses. The sectors represented by the participants included (a) recreational, (b) service, (c) retail, (d) housing, (e), transportation, and (f) restaurant.

Demographics and Biological Data

The demographics of the participants consisted of two attributes: (a) gender and (b) age. First, gender attribute included seven females and three males (60% and 40% respectively). The age attribute consisted of seven (70%) of the participants aged between 18 to 49 and three (30%) of the participants aged 50 and above.

Table 1

Demographic features of the study Participants - Gender

Gender	Number of Matching Nodes	Percentage (%)
Unassigned	0	0
Not Applicable	0	0
Male	3	30
Female	7	70

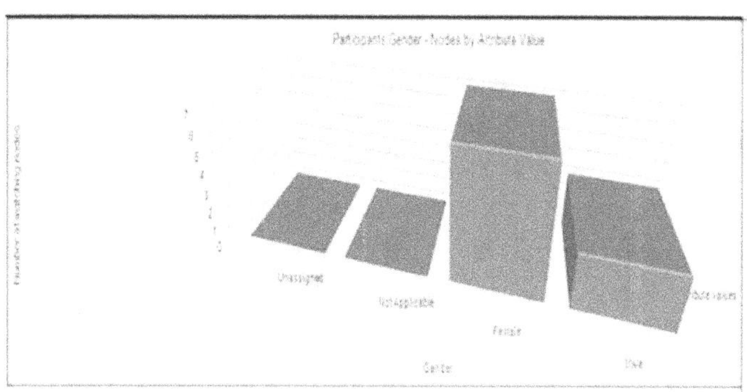

Figure 1. Chart - Demographic features of the study Participants - Gender

Table 2

Demographic features of the study Participants - Age

Age	Number of matching nodes	Percentage (%)
18 – 30	1	10
31 – 40	1	10
41 – 49	1	10
50 – Above	7	70

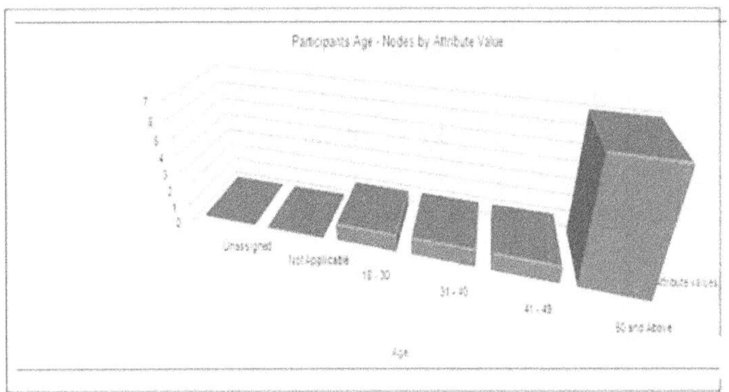

Figure 2. Chart - Demographic features of the study Participants - Age.

From the 250 letters mailed to potential participants, 25 expressed real interest in participating in the study, 31 did not have up-to-date information, 60 did not respond, and 100 either were not willing to participate or did not have a direct experience concerning the failure of small businesses. It was difficult finding potential participants committing to one-on-one interviews because of conflicting private life and work schedules. Two of the participants requested to be recorded in the follow-up one-on-one interview to discuss further the research topic of failure of small businesses in detail. The subsequent interviews were consistent with the already collected data and did not yield new information.

Pilot Study

The determination of the creditability of the study findings and interpretation was attained through instrument validation that involved a survey of interviews and performing of a pilot study. The researcher utilized the pilot study purposely to (a) achieve interview questions' appropriateness and clarity, (b) establish whether the questions would result in significant responses, and (c) allow making conclusions about the study's impact (Creswell, 2005; Neuman, 2006). The feedback from the questions used in the pilot study was assessed, and inconsequential modifications were proposed and integrated into the final format. The interview questions were insignificantly reworded for clarity improvement and allowed the participants answer the questions more direct (Neuman, 2006). The format and interview questions were unaltered for the participants did not recommend a need for any improvement. The final version of the interview questions (IQ) is given in Appendix A.

The pilot study entailed three selected participants who were excluded from the main research. The selection and interviewing of the participants was initiated after IRB approval of the study's proposal. Letters of invitation were mailed to the potential participants requesting for involvement in the study.

Purposive sampling was used in selecting the participants

to be involved in the pilot study. The selection to participate criteria included small businesses owner leaders who must (a) have operated the business for at least five years, (b) employed between zero and 50 workers, and (c) exceeded reasonable expectations. The participants interviewed owned the businesses in across varied sectors and no data analysis was conducted.

Review of Data Collection

The qualitative intrinsic phenomenological study was conducted in three stages:
(a)   interview questions development, (b) pilot testing, and (c) collecting data. First, the development of interview questions involved the central research question used to guide the research. Some interview questions were used to cover any excluded questions or to add any viewpoint significant to the study. Pilot testing was the second stage that involved collecting the data from three participants using the research question and personal interview.

The third stage was the data collection. Before the start of an interview, every research participant was asked to sign the informed consent form document (see Appendix B). The contents of the form included the; (a) rights of participants to participate voluntarily or decline to respond to any questions, (b) duration of participation, (c) participation consent, and (d) details about the confidentiality of the data collected (Cooper & Schindler, 2003).

Data collection duration was 90 days with every initial interview lasting between 30 and 60 minutes. Averagely, initial interviews lasted for 45 minutes. Ten personal interviews were conducted, and three participants were requested to participate in a 15-minute follow-up interviews. The study involved three follow-up telephone interviews for the researcher to attain clarity on the initial responses.

After pilot testing, the first initial interview of the participant was on September 18, 2015. The reviewing process of qualifications of the participants, scheduling, interviewing and transcribing of audio recorded interviews continued until (a) the end of the last participant was interviewed on November 30, 2015, and (b) final interview transcripts were completed on December 15, 2015. The duration for collecting the data was 125 days.

Interview Process

The study involved conducting one-on-one interviews based on schedules and the location identified. The researcher began interviewing the participants by reminding interviewees of confidentiality of the responses and that no right or wrong answers to the questions existed. Furthermore, the participants were reminded about the recording of the interviews and that the dissertation copies and transcripts from the interview would be provided upon request.

Four of the participants requested a copy of the transcript from the interviews. Four of the participants requested a copy of the completed dissertation. The requested transcripts were mailed and received within a day of the interview. The researcher confirmed sending the requested copies through telephone and asked the participants to review and indicate the transcripts as accepted or advise of any anomaly or inaccuracies. The researcher requested the participant to respond within five days from time received or otherwise the transcripts would be assumed to be accurate. Figure 3 is used to illustrate the interview process adopted.

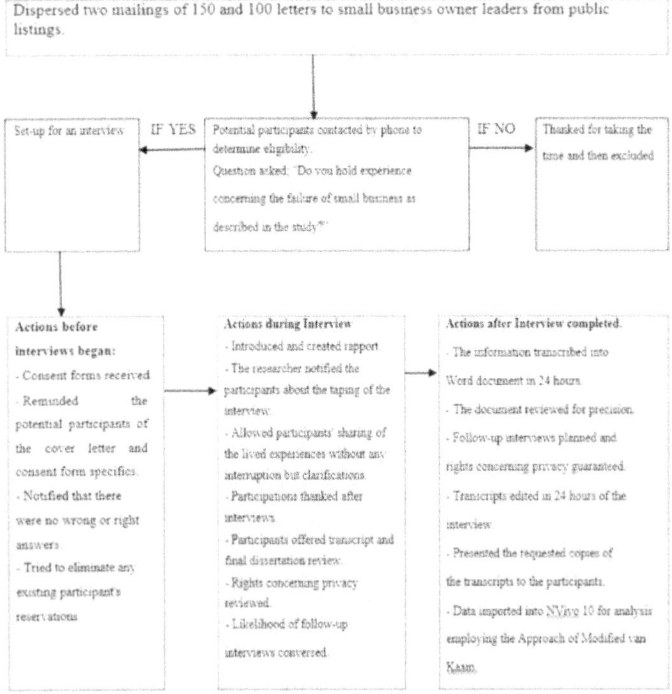

Figure 3. Visual Presentation of the Interview Process

The Process of Data Analysis

The data gathered from the participants' interviews as audio recording were qualitatively analyzed. The in-depth interviews resulted in 70 pages of the data and transcribed in Microsoft Word. The researcher conducted three cross-references of the audio recorded interviews against the data transcribed to eliminate bias and affirm the accuracy of the transcription.

Upon the accuracy confirmation of the transcribed data from the interviews, copies of the transcripts were mailed to each participant respectively. The participants were requested to make comments, changes or approve the respective interviews transcribed in five days. If no feedback was received within the specified period, the information was regarded accurate and therefore applied in the study. Five participants responded within five days and requested minor changes to the data transcribed and approved the data. Two participants approved the data transcribed via mail, two of the participants used the telephone to approve the information transcribed, and the last one was considered accurate since the participant did not respond to the approval request in 5 days.

The transcribed interviews were uploaded into NVivo 10, the software utilized for data analysis in qualitative research. The data were bracketed, coded into themes, analyzed, and led to answers to the central research question as reported in Chapter 4. The NVivo10 was used to compare the data from the transcribed interviews to recognize similarities, patterns repeated, and themes. Furthermore, data bracketing and coding into themes allowed identification of data contrast.

To enhance the reliability of the research, the processes of collecting and analyzing the data complied with creditability, dependability, confirmability, and transferability as follows. Dependability was used to refer to audit-trailing to establish the data origin, how collected and used. In the main and pilot studies, the data were collected from the in-depth interviews that were recorded, transcribed, analyzed and applied to answer the research question. Creditability was used to refer to the reliability of the findings of the data, recognizing the mostly shared themes from the participants to analyze the data transcribed and the similarities coded. Transferability was used to refer to the possibility of future duplicating or using the results of the study. The results from the research, the applied data collection, and analysis processes may be replicated in various framework or population that aligns with the current study's criteria. Confirmability is used when the data, findings, and results of the study apply to future study or new research.

The participants' feedback from the pilot study had allowed the refining of interview questions before the actual study interviews took place. The adjustment involved insignificant re-wording of interview questions for clarity improvement and allowed the participants answer the questions more direct (Neuman, 2006). The interview questions were used to stimulate responses effectively in answering the research question. The possibility to expand the data, findings and results meant that the study attained the confirmability.

The purpose of contrasting and comparing the collected data from the reports was to achieve a comprehensive insight of the participants' lived experiences. Numerous reports were created in NVivo 10 by using interview questions and following in-depth interviewing protocol (see Appendix A). Every question used in the in-depth interview protocol was uploaded into NVivo 10 with the responses from participants to each of the questions.

After uploading the interview data for analysis, running a query ensued to identify the frequencies of phrase and word within every question, compared amongst the participants and coded to relate the data to the research question. The themes recognized as commonly shared by the participants were grouped as prevalent themes. The researcher affirmed the accuracy of the identified prevalent themes in NVivo 10 and well documented in the interviews transcribed.

Modified van Kaam Approach

The study was designed utilizing the approach of modified van Kaam to enhance an understanding of the phenomenon (Moustakas, 1996) failure of small businesses. A structured design was utilized in the study to obtain an insight into the problem, which involved eliminating previous judgments or assumptions and concentrated on obtaining unique and unbiased outcomes (Blum & Muirhead, 2005; Moustakas, 1994). According to Moustakas (1994), the modified van Kaam approach involved the following specific steps for analyzing the data:

1.Preliminary listing and grouping.

2.Reduction and exclusion.

3.Invariant constituent clustering or grouping and thematization.

4.Constituent (invariant) identification and theme application.

5.Textural description of each participant's lived experience, applying relevant variant constituents and themes.

6.Structural experience construction for every individual co-researcher was relying on personal variations in imaginations and textural descriptions.

7.Textural structure construction for every research participant, describing the meanings and significance of lived experiences.

8.Constituent (variant) and theme integration. (pp. 121-122)

The specific steps from the van Kaam Modified approach are described visually and presented in Figure 4.

Step 6: Structural experience construction for every individual co-researcher relying on his or her personal variations in imaginations and textural descriptions.

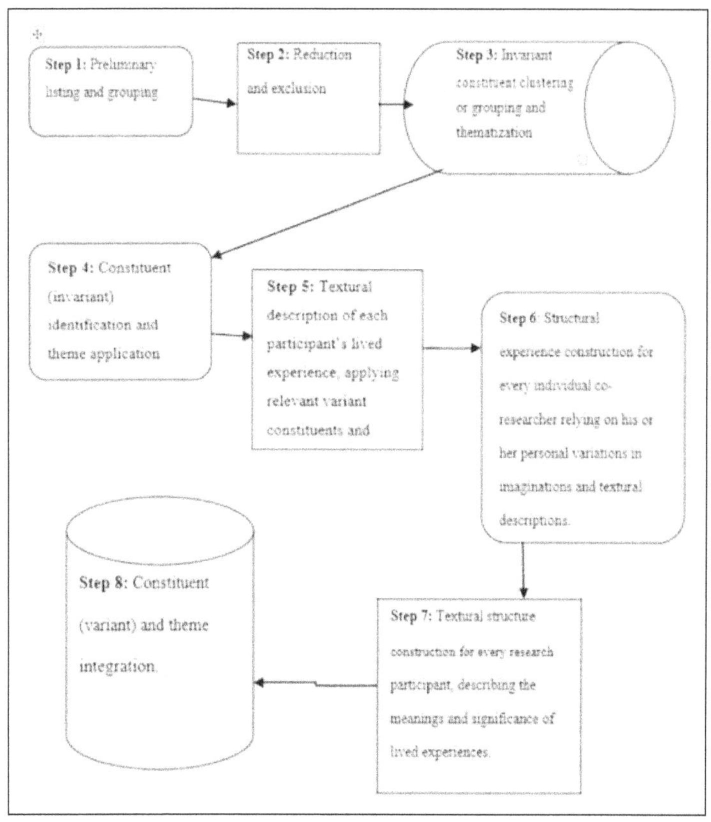

Figure 4. Steps used for analyzing the Data.

Horizonalization

According to Moustakas (1994), every horizon was used to provide a phenomenon's clear view. In the current study, the study participants offered a perfect view of the failure of small businesses. Horizonalization process involved coding the data into categories with repetitive reflective analysis to uncover rich themes. The first explicit step in horizonalization of data analysis was to review every interview question for important sentences, statements, or quotations to gain the insight (Creswell, 2007) of how small business owner leaders experienced failure of small businesses. The verbally recorded interviews for the 10 participants were transcribed and downloaded into NVivo 10 to help in managing and analyzing the data.

The auto coded data in NVivo 10 were used in coding every interview question to discover broader themes. The codes in NVivo were used to review every question within the transcripts for connected statements, experiences, or ideas, followed by theme reviewing and coding. Basit (2003) argued that coding and analyzing were un-synonymous though coding was a critical element of analysis. Table 3 was used to illustrate relevant expressions out of shared experiences.

Table 3

Horizonalization: Relevant Expressions

Leaders need to know	Personality and presentation	Know how to
Motivate and recognize employees	Ensure resources are utilized	Be captain
Have the knowledge	Understand the role	Look for the area
Training	Manage and operate business successfully	Meet regularly
Polite, knowledgeable	Understand the role	Do not educate
Want to be authoritarian	Leadership most important	People who work for them
Small business has to succeed	Greet clientele	Honest and trustworthy
Believe in the ability	Bad government regulations	Educate through bachelor's
Power to understand	Know how to talk	Understand the location

Word cloud is constructed from the word frequency query and is used to refer to the most commonly used words in the data (Lee et al., 2010). In the current study, the larger the word in the word cloud means the word was more frequently used by the participants. Lee et al. (2010) argued that the largest word size meant most frequently used the word while the smallest word in size is the one least used by the participants during the interviews as illustrated in Figure 5. Researchers use word frequency to analyze interviews and make sense of the data allowing theme construction (Lee et al., 2010). Figure 5 is a diagram of the word cloud from the participants' interviews in the current study.

Figure 5. Word Frequency Query - Word Cloud.

Tree-Map

Figure 6 is a tree-map that was used to illustrate the visualization involved in computing and information (Shneiderman

& Plaisant, 2009).). In the current study, tree mapping was an approach used to display data in a hierarchical manner by nesting the rectangles. Shneiderman and Plaisant, (2009) argued that the rectangle nodes contain areas proportional to particular data dimensions separated as illustrated in Figure 6.

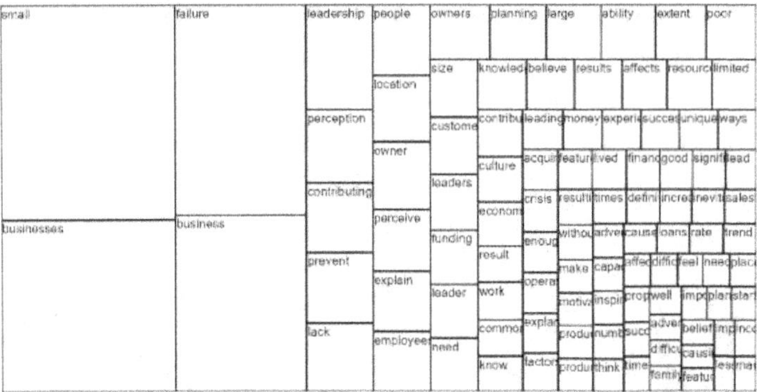

Figure 6. Word Frequency Query - Tree Map.

Findings

The purpose of this qualitative phenomenological intrinsic study was to explore the perceptions and meaning of small business owner leaders' experiences concerning the failure of small businesses. The participation of 10 small business owner leaders resulted in emerging of nine themes from the responses. The themes included: lack of funding, limited resources; lack of knowledge and understanding; poor or lack of leadership; economic crisis or underdevelopment of the economy; poor business location; lack of motivation and inspiration; culture; size; and poor planning. The constructs of themes in the current qualitative study represented the perceptions and contexts of the ten small business owner leaders sharing the experiences of small business failure.

Reduction and Elimination

Reductions and eliminations required analyzing of the expressions relevant, coding as nodes into NVivo 10 to determine suitable groupings of themes. The researcher tested every expression relevant using the approach of Modified van Kaam method to determine if the following requirements were obtained; (a) reflecting the lived experience depiction both as necessary and sufficient component of understanding (Moustakas, 1994) failure of small businesses and (b) whether it would be abstracted (Moustakas, 1994) and labeled or grouped afterward. The expressions that met the two conditions qualified as experience horizons and constituents that were variant (Moustakas, 1994). The ones that did not meet the requirements were automatically eliminated.

The researcher grouped the repetitive expressions singly into the nodes according to Modified Van Kaam Method (Moustakas, 1994). Moustakas (1994) argued that unclear expressions were considered irrelevant in enhancing failure of small businesses' phenomenon and therefore either presented in clearer terms or removed from the process of analysis. Expressions were presented in clearer terms by offering more explanations without changing the participants' intended meaning. The intended meaning was relied on when stating vague expressions in precise terms.

In case the participants offered strange expressions,

phrases or examples to people who did not own small businesses, clarification was necessary. The extra clarification or explanation was carefully done to sustain a match with initial interview transcripts offered. If the match of new expressions used in clarification did not align with the transcripts, elimination from the analysis was necessary. Analyzing using NVivo 10 software enhanced grouping of thematically relevant expressions across interview questions. The software allowed connection of participants' responses to every emerging theme.

Clustering of the Main Themes

Reviewing of the invariant constituents resulted in emerging of shared patterns of significance about the failure of the small business phenomenon. The ones with a shared thematic foundation were clustered. Moustakas (1994) argued clustering of the invariant constituents allowed the recognition of themes of the core experience. The analysis resulted in nine major themes as listed following the order of significance; 1. Lack of funding and limited resources, 2. Lack of knowledge and understanding, 3. Poor leadership involving not people-oriented, poor and business operations, 4. Economic crisis including economic underdevelopment, 5. Poor business location that is un-strategic, 6. Lack of motivation and inspiration, 7. Culture, 8. Size, and 9. Poor Planning.

Either one of the following two factors were used to guide the selection of the core themes (a) theme occurred throughout the interview questions, or (b) theme was frequently referenced by two or more participants. The themes that satisfied both factors were noted, such as emphasized on poor leadership, limited resource and lack of knowledge. The themes of limited resources and lack of knowledge emerged from eight participants (80%) and eight participants (80%), respectively. Other emerging themes included:

The theme of poor or lack leadership was mentioned by seven participants (70%) followed by economic crisis (five participant - 50%), poor business location (four participants - 40%), lack of motivation and inspiration (three participants - 30%), culture (three participants - 30%), small- sized in nature (two participants - 20%) and poor planning (two participants - 20%).

Last Step of Invariant Constituents and Themes Identified and Textual Descriptors.

The terminal identification of invariant constituents and aligned themes were motivated by factors of expressed explicitly within the transcripts from the interview and investigated the compatibility of invariant constituents and themes if the explicit expression of the transcripts from interview did not exist (Moustakas, 1994). The analysis resulted in the elimination of the invariant constituents and aligned themes neither expressed explicitly within transcripts from the interview nor compatible.

The responses of the participants were recognized by interviewees' numbers. Added to the number of interviewees were textual descriptors used to describe experiences of the participants. Tables 4 to 38 represent the application of NVivo10 to analyze the interview questions, emerging themes, numbers of participants and descriptions.

Cluster and Textural Descriptions of Themes

Reduction and elimination of the central research question resulted in emerging of two main and three minor themes used to explain the phenomenon. The themes mentioned by the Participants in order of significance included lack of funding and limited resources, poor leadership, lack of knowledge, poor customer service and government regulations as illustrated in Tables 4 - 8.

Table 4
Failure of small businesses can be caused by lack of funding and limited resources

Emerging theme	Participants
Failure of small businesses can be caused by lack of funding and limited resources.	3, 5, 9, 10

Textual Description - Small businesses lack enough finances for product promotion. According to the Participants, Small businesses lack necessary funds for advertising and branding; cannot afford to pay specialized employees, bad credit, lack of collateral security and therefore banks perceive them as risky for loans, no enough time as much is spent on family welfare, depend on inefficient family labor and difficulty in acquiring insurance. Most participants mentioned Poor leadership as the cause of failure of small businesses as illustrated in Table 5.

Table 5

Failure of small businesses can be caused by poor leadership.

Textual description / Theme	Participants
Emerging theme - Failure of small businesses can be caused by poor leadership.	1, 2, 3, 6

Textual Description - In the participants' discussions, poor leadership was associated with poor leadership style and lack of vision. According to the Participants, poor leadership is associated with, lack of prior leadership experiences, unable to lead people, poor employee management, unable to take employees' constructive feedback and no action plan respectively. Harrison and Parish (2008) argued that failing in duties resulted from the lack of leadership and the inability to sustain superior performance standards.

According to Harrison and Parish (2008), followers were discouraged from making honest contribution and criticisms by inferior quality correspondences characterized by high level of insensitivity, misinformation, and misleading. Poor communication results in delays and ultimate failure of small businesses (Harrison & Parish, 2008). The theme of lack of knowledge emerged as one of the contributors to the failure of the small businesses as illustrated in Table 6.

Table 6

Failure of small businesses may be caused by lack of knowledge and skills.

Theme	Participants
Emerging theme - Failure of small businesses may be caused by lack of knowledge and skills.	Participants 3, 4

Textual description - Participant 2 mentioned a lack of business awareness and knowledge of the product, business plan, a place to sell and culture complicates understanding of the business. Small business owners need basic business education, classes, seminars, training, and skills to prevent failure of small businesses (Participant 4). Lack of knowledge results in poor resource allocation, poor communication, customer services, and loss of sales resulted in the failure of small businesses. Without knowledge, small business owners may not know how to start, operate and sustain the business effectively (Participant 4).

Table 7
Failure of small businesses can be caused by poor customer service.

Textual description / Theme
Emerging theme - Failure of small businesses Participants 3, 4 can be caused by poor customer service.

Textual description - Lack of customer services result in failure of small businesses. Customers are turned off when businesses lack products to sell, unwelcoming to customers, goods not strategically placed and paying no attention to the customer's demand. The situation results in loss of sales and ultimate closing of the businesses.

Government policy and regulations contributed to the failure of the small businesses as illustrated in Table 8.

Table 8
Failure of small businesses can be cause by government policy and regulations

Theme	Participants
Failure of small businesses can be cause by government policy and regulations	5, 7

Textual description - The participants described how government policies are used to regulate, restrict and limit small business operations enhancing problems of small businesses. Lack of government subsidies, high taxes inhibit prosperity of small businesses. Also when governmental officials prohibit large businesses from buying out small businesses, failure is the only option at times of financial crisis.

The clustering of original emerging themes discerned from Interview Question 1 reduction and elimination stage resulted in two main themes and one minor theme. The main themes were mentioned by four participants each, and the minor theme was supported by three participants. The three themes were clustered as lack of resources and limited funding, lack of knowledge and awareness, and lack of advertisement as illustrated in Tables 9 to 11.

Table 9
Failure of small businesses can be caused by lack of resources and limited funding.

Theme	Participants
Failure of small businesses can be caused by lack of resources and limited funding.	4, 5, 6, 7

Textual description - Participant 4 said, "Time is vital to small businesses, and I decided to venture into small business without resources, such as labor and capital. I was unemployed when I decided to start the small business." Participant 5 commented that "small businesses lack finance. We small business owners do not have enough money to start and operate businesses successfully."

Failure of small businesses occurs because owners do not have more money, many customers and not well established compared to large businesses (Participant 6). Participant 7 said, "Small business is owner's sacrifice of time and family labor, which the family needs most for quality time. If the owner of a small business does not sacrifice and dedicate the most needed quality family time and resources, the business will inevitably fail." Lack of knowledge and awareness was also another emerging theme that contributed to the failure of small businesses as illustrated in Table 10.

Table 10
Failure of small businesses can be caused by lack of knowledge and awareness

Theme	Participants
Failure of small businesses can be caused by lack of resources and limited funding.	4, 5, 6, 7

Textual description - Participant 1 said, "most customers are unaware of small businesses' products." In agreement, Participant 4 said that,

"To ensure I succeeded in my small business, I took

businesses classes where I learned about business plans, marketing, areas needed to establish a business without which small business can fail. I started attending every business seminar when I was overwhelmed as a small business owner."

The emerging theme of lack of advertisement is illustrated in Table 11.

Table 11

Failure of small businesses can be caused by lack of advertisement

Theme	Participants
Emerging theme - Failure of small businesses can be caused by lack of advertisement.	1, 5, 10

Textual description - Participant 1 said, "Lack of advertisement and labor is a common feature in small businesses that contribute to failure. It is expensive to pay running costs, such as advertisement and wages and salaries when business is not generating sufficient income." Concurring with Participant 1, Participant 5 asserted that lack of advertisement characterized in small businesses contributed to failure because customers could not easily trace the business location. Furthermore, Participant 10 said,

If I advertised the product to create awareness, I would have done better. I was not motivated to do well because I did not try to market as the product was selling by itself. If I advertised the product to create awareness, I would have done better. I lost clientele because of lack of advertising and lost huge sales as I retired from teaching and my coworkers were the large part of my customers. Continued selling to the customers who only contacted me and not too many people contacted me that resulted in the failure of my business.

The clustering of original emerging themes discerned from Interview Question 2 reduction and elimination stage resulted in four themes. The emerging themes listed in order of significance included lack of resources and limited funding, lack of knowledge, limited market or unfavorable competition and poor business location as illustrated in Tables 12- 15.

Table 12
Failure of small businesses can be caused by lack resources and limited Resources.

Emerging theme	Participants
Failure of small businesses can be caused by lack resources and limited Resources.	4, 6, 7, 9, 10

Textual Description: "Small businesses fail because of lack of resources. Small businesses are limited with proper contact with right individuals and information to know the status and direction of the businesses" (Participant 4). Unlike large businesses that succeed, small businesses lack sufficient enough money for advertising or marketing, do not afford more products for sales, which results in reduced profits and failure (Participant 5). Participant 7 said,

> "Sometimes owners of small businesses draw proceeds from small businesses for their personal expenses when their personal incomes are not enough. Owners of small businesses do not have enough income to spend and

therefore draw much of the proceeds from small businesses to sustain personal financial demands."

Participant 10 supported participant's idea that "Unlike small businesses, large businesses have more finances, more people working, specialized supporting departments such as public relations, and human resources". Lack of knowledge was the other emerging theme that contributed to the failure of small as illustrated in Table 13.

Table 13
Failure of small businesses can be caused by lack of knowledge

Emerging Theme	Participants
Failure of small businesses can be caused by lack of knowledge	1, 4

Textural Description: Participant 1 said, "when products are new in the market, it is harder to get people try what they are not familiar or used to and sticking to it (loyalty)." Small businesses are limited with proper contact, right individuals and information to know the status and direction of the businesses (Participant 4). Participants 5 and 6 mentioned the unfavorable competition and the other theme that contributed to the failure of small businesses as seen in Table 25.

Table 14

Failure of small businesses can be caused by unfavorable competition.

Emerging theme	Participants
Failure of small businesses can be caused by unfavorable competition.	5, 6

Textual Description: - The number of customers is limited because of market competition (Participant 5). Participant 6 added that "Unlike small businesses that result in failure, large businesses have enough money for competing through advertising or marketing, afford more products for sales resulting in increased profits." Participants 6 and 9 mentioned the theme of poor location contributing to the failure of small businesses as illustrated in Table 15.

Table 15

Failure of small businesses can be caused by poor location.

Emerging theme	Participants
Failure of small businesses can be caused by poor location.	6, 9.

Textural Description: Not strategic, inaccessible result in failure of small businesses (Participant 6). Participant 6 commented that "unlike large businesses, my small business I did not have a permanent address from where to direct the customers." Participant 9 said that "Back to assessment, a small business located in a strategically wrong area results in failure."

The clustering of original emerging themes discerned from

Interview Question 3 reduction and elimination stage resulted in one main theme and two minor themes. The main theme of lack or limited resources and funding is illustrated in Table 16.

Table 16

Failure of small businesses can be caused by limited resources and funding

Emerging theme	Participants
Failure of small businesses can be caused by limited resources and funding.	1, 4, 6, 7

Textural Description: - No enough client resulting in insufficient revenue, unaware of business status, bills more than generated income from sales result in failure (Participant 1). Participant 4 said, "high cost of living for small business owners, lack the time and of assistance from family members and friends can lead to failure of small businesses." Participant 6 commented that,

Small businesses fail because the owners do not have the right tools, such as employees and the available ones may not be informed to know the business status like in large businesses, and are operated everywhere/ unstable. Small businesses are always struggling because it is harder to secure loans, unlike large businesses. Unlike large businesses with stakeholders, small business owners are the only self-partners of the businesses that cause capital limitation and failure of the business. Lack of knowledge was the first emerging minor theme that contributed to the failure of small businesses as illustrated in Table 17.

Table 17

Failure of small business can be caused by lack of knowledge.

Textural Description / Theme	Participants
Emerging theme - Failure of small business can be caused by lack of knowledge	1, 4, 6

Textural Description: - Participant 1 suggested that "No enough clienteles, unaware of business status, bills more than income generated from sales resulted in failure." Limited knowledge about the small business industry by the people who operate small businesses, such as friends and family members contribute to small business failure (Participant 4). Participant 6 said that "small businesses fail because the owners do not have the right tools, such as knowledgeable employees to know the business status like in large businesses." Table 18 is used to illustrate the second emerging minor theme of high operating costs contributing to the failure of small businesses.

Table 18

Failure of small businesses can be caused by high operating costs

Emerging Theme	Participants
High operating costs	1, 4, 7

Textural Description: - Participant 1 said that failure of small businesses happens as the business operations result in more bills than the income generated from sales leading to in failure. Owners of small businesses draw finances from businesses to meet high personal expenses that result from a high cost of living (Participant 4). Participant 7 agreed when that commented,

Sometimes owners of small businesses draw proceeds from small businesses for their personal expenses when their personal incomes are not enough. Owners of small businesses do not have enough income to spend and therefore draw much of the proceeds from small businesses to sustain personal financial demands.

The clustering of original emerging themes discerned from Interview Question 4 reduction and elimination stage resulted in two themes, one main and the other minor. Lack of knowledge, education and Training were clustered as the main theme supported by five participants (50%) as illustrated in Table 19.

Table 19
Failure of small businesses is caused by lack of knowledge, education, and training.

Emerging theme	Participant
Failure of small businesses is caused by lack of knowledge, education, and training	1, 5, 6, 9, 10

Textural Description: - Owners of small businesses lack leadership training (Participant, 1). Participant 9 agreed when commented,
"First of all, if a person is not trained or not worked in businesses may cause failure. The person may lack prior leadership skills, not know how to talk to people, train

employees, meet and greet clienteles."

Participant 5 said,
>"most leaders do not have the knowledge of handling the business. The owner leaders of small businesses need to understand how to manage the business. You can manage a business without knowing you are making losses until business collapses."

A leader has to know the products well and where to sell (Participant 6). Participant 10 concurred when commented, "A leader needs to be knowledgeable about what is happening around the business, follow through and stick to it. I was not hustling to succeed." Lack of leadership and previous experiences was clustered as the minor theme as was supported by four (40%) participants as illustrated in Table 20.

Table 20

Failure of small businesses can be caused by lack of leadership and prior experiences

Textural description / theme	Participants
Emerging theme - Failure of small businesses can be caused by lack of leadership and prior experiences	1, 4, 6, 9

Textural Description: Participant 1 said that "most owners of small businesses have not held leadership positions and starting to lead people will be a little harder because of the owners' views about what constitutes proper leadership." Poor leadership such as self or inward looking leadership is not driven, have closed doors to opinions and new ideas resulting in failure (Participant 4).

Participant 6 said,

> You have to be a leader when in business to make profits and minimize losses. A leader has to know the products well and the place to sell, communicate the business' mission to employees. A leader must be able to work with employees and customers, trusted to fulfill the promises, advice in advance if not going to fulfill the promises, and must be a good communicator to customers. Lack of all these will result in failure of small businesses.

First of all, failure may occur if owners of small businesses lack training or past work experience in businesses. The person may lack prior leadership skills, not know how to talk to people, train employees, meet and greet clienteles. Also, some leaders want to be authoritarian and look down upon employees contributing to the failure of small businesses (Participant 9).

The originally emerging themes were clustered from Interview Question 5 reduction and elimination stage into one theme. Lack of knowledge, education and training emerged and clustered as the main theme as was supported by six participants (60%) as illustrated in Table 21.

Table 21

Failure of small businesses can be caused by lack of knowledge and lack of education and training.

Textural description / theme	Participants
Emerging theme - Failure of small businesses can be caused by lack of knowledge and lack of education and training	3, 4, 5, 6, 9, 10

Textural Description: Lack of knowledge has a lot of impacts. One needs to know the product, where to sell it, at least area code, accommodating customers instead of saying "I don't know" (Participant 3). Participant 10 commented:

You cannot start a business if you do not have enough knowledge about the business. There is the need to go for training, workshops, reading extensively to know what is needed. Some succeed because they are already in the business area, but others need training and workshops to succeed. According to Participant 4:

> Lack of knowledge is a huge contributor to the failure of small businesses. There are places to get knowledge and without proper knowledge, resources and time is a huge hindrance. There are immense knowledge to gain if you know proper sources and areas. I did not take college business classes but nonprofit making based classes that had contact with the city and city leaders. I had unlimited knowledge but did not invest my time in the right people for help, and this resulted in the failure of my small business.

Sometimes we need the knowledge to start and handle business. Lack of business understanding creates a need to knowledge (Participant 5). Participant 6 said, "Lack of knowledge is when you get business with no idea of your customers. Small business owners need to know the market very well. It is important for people to make sense of the business without which business fails".

"As far as leadership is concerned, you need to know the

business to lead. Without knowledge, you cannot lead. To be a leader, one could have training, take classes, and be able to bring something to the table." (Participant 9).

The originally emerging themes were clustered from Interview Question 6 reduction and elimination stage into two main themes and one minor theme. Lack of knowledge was the first of the two main themes supported by 4 Participants as illustrated in Table 22.

Table 22

Failure of small businesses can be caused by lack of knowledge, education, training and poor resources allocation

Emerging theme	Participants
Failure of small businesses can be caused by lack of knowledge, education, training and poor resources allocation	3, 4, 7, 9

Textural Description - According to Participant 3, knowledgeable and caring about customers and business impacted the ability to prevent failure of small businesses. Participant 4 said, "Going out and acquiring information will contribute toward the success of a small business to prevent failure." Participant 7 commented that assigning employees to specific and ideal jobs, reduced confusion and enhanced the understanding of roles and duties preventing failure of small businesses. "Again leaders need to know how to talk to employees, subordinates, and customers, understanding and compassionate to peoples' problems and assume the leadership role" (Participant 9). The second main theme that emerged was the lack of leadership, vision, action plan, honesty, motivation and inspiration, supported by 4 participants as illustrated in Table 23.

Table 23

Failure of small businesses can be caused by the lack of leadership vision, pro-activeness, motivation, and inspiration

Textural description / theme	Participants
Failure of small businesses can be caused by the lack of leadership vision, pro-activeness, motivation, and inspiration	3, 4, 6, 9

Textural Description: Being honest as leaders, personable, polite, knowledgeable, good personality, presentation, and care about customers and businesses impact the leader's capacity to prevent failure of small businesses (Participant 3). Participant 4 said, "Being proactive as a leader is surrounding myself with the right people." According to Participant 6:

What you need to know is the future of the business and how to project. As owner-leader of the small business, you need to stop and reevaluate to see what went wrong when you realize things are not going well. Do not wait till there is huge deep or losses to make changes. Failure to analyze and evaluation of the business early enough results to failure.

Participant 9 said:

Again leaders need to know how to talk to employees, subordinates, and customers, understanding and compassionate to peoples' problems and assume the leadership role. Also as a leader, you need to recognize people who work for you. You need to offer training, skills, and more positive comments and less focus on the negative side.

The theme of misallocation of resources was supported by 2 participants as illustrated in Tables 24.

Table 24

Failure of small businesses can be caused by misallocation of resources

Textural Description	Participants
Emerging theme - Failure of small businesses can be caused by misallocation of resources	4, 7

Textural Description - Leaders proactively surround themselves with the right people (Participant 4). Participant 7 said, "good leadership means staying on budget. Poor leadership overstretches the business budget from over-recruiting employees, not assigning employees to specific and ideal jobs, leads to confusion, and lack of understanding of roles and duties."

The originally emerging themes from Interview Question 7 reductions and elimination stage were clustered into two major themes supported by four participants each and two minor ones supported by two participants each. The first emerging main theme was the lack of resources and limited funding difficulties. The theme was supported by four participants as illustrated in Table 25.

Table 25

Failure of small businesses can cause lack of resources and funding difficulties

Textural description / theme	Participants
Emerging theme - Failure of small businesses can cause lack of resources and funding difficulties	5, 6, 9, 10

Textural Description: - Participant 5 said:Yes, increasing failure rate trend is killing the economy. When small businesses are failing in mass level, people do not pay taxes and therefore the government lacks the money needed for development and public service. I stopped paying taxes when my business failed.

Participant 6 said:

> You know what, I think small businesses have a big part to play in the economy. Small businesses are well supporting the economy and a lot of people through employment, able to pay taxes, and support families. Failure of small businesses results in the lack of money to support families, kids, employees, pay taxes and poor economy.

"Yes, the decline of small businesses result in less money in the community served or economy, and eventually small businesses close down"(Participant 9). Participant 10 said, "Increasing failure rates results in no enough money to rotate back to the system. More lucrative businesses promote the economy, but failing businesses hurt." Second, the underdevelopment of the economy was also clustered as the main theme each supported by the Participants 1, 4, 5, and 10 as illustrated in Table 26.

Table 26

Failure of small businesses may result in search underdevelopment of the economy and low living standards

Emerging theme:	Participants
Failure of small businesses may result in search underdevelopment of the economy and low living standards	1, 4, 5, 10

Textural Descriptions: - Participant 1 said, "I think yes because most small businesses are opened out of loans and high failure rates inevitably affect the economy adversely."

"I think high failure rates are affecting the economy because people who are trying to build something cannot get off the ground as large entities consume the market and prevent small businesses from thriving"(Participant 4). Participant 5 said:

Yes, increasing failure rate trend is killing the economy. When small businesses are failing in mass level, people do not pay taxes and therefore the government lacks the money needed for development and public service. I stopped paying taxes when my business failed. Business success results in increased economic activities as more money circulates and increased ability to pay taxes. Participant 10 said, "Increasing failure rates results in no enough money to rotate back to the system. More lucrative businesses promote the economy, but failing businesses hurt the economy." Participants 6 and 9 supported the first minor theme clustered as unemployment as illustrated in Table 27.

Table 27

Failure of small businesses may be caused by unemployment

Emerging theme:	Participants
Failure of small businesses may be caused by unemployment.	6, 9

Textural Description - Participant 6 said, "I think small businesses have a big part to play in the economy. Small businesses are well supporting the economy and a lot of people through employment. Failure of small businesses results in the lack of money to support employees." "When sales of the product decline at times of economic crisis find a way to reverse this situation to increase the sales and maybe cut employees' working hours" (Participant 9). Participants 5 and 6 supported the second minor theme clustered as low tax revenue as illustrated in Table 28.

Table 28

Failure of small businesses may be caused by low Tax revenue

Emerging theme:	Participants
Failure of small businesses may result in low Tax revenue	5, 6

Textural Descriptions - "When small businesses are failing in mass level, people do not pay taxes and therefore the government lacks the money needed for development and public service. I stopped paying taxes when my business failed" (Participant 5).

Participant 6 said, "small businesses are well supporting the economy and a lot of people through employment, able to pay taxes, and support families."

The originally emerging themes from Interview Question 8 reductions and elimination stage were clustered into one major theme. The theme of lack or poor leadership included not knowing how to lead people, unable to reinforce policies and poor decision making. A half of the participants interviewed responded to the theme of poor leadership as illustrated in Table 29.

Table 29

Failure of small businesses can be caused by poor leadership including bad decision-making, inability to lead, and reinforce business policies and not people-oriented.

Textural description / theme	Participants
Emerging theme - Failure of small businesses can be caused by poor leadership including bad decision-making, inability to lead, and reinforce business policies and not people-oriented.	3, 4, 6, 9, 10.

Textural Description: - Participant 3 said, "I think it is significant. Somebody has to lead, head, and lay rules before having people come in to work for success." Participant 4 asserted:

I perceive leadership as important because there has to be a leader well informed to hold everything together. Otherwise, everything fails. A business that lacks proper leadership will not get off the ground. Lack of leadership would enable other competitors to take over the market share and ground your business that results in failure.

In agreement, Participant 6 commented that "Small businesses require strong leadership to lead the businesses to make profits and lead people effectively. Poor leaders cannot lead people adequately resulting in the failure of the businesses."

According to Participant 9:

Leadership is very significant because business problems start and intensify if you do not have proper leadership. The downturn of the economy, business, control of inventory, and invoices are not possible without proper leadership. Lack of leadership will affect the business adversely.

The originally emerging themes from Interview Question 9 reductions and elimination stage were clustered into one major theme and two minor themes. The leaders' ability to motivate and inspire resulted in the emerging of a major theme. The emphasis on the theme was employees feeling motivated or appreciated. Table 30 was used to illustrate the main theme.

Table 30

Failure of small businesses could be caused by inability of a leader to motivate and inspire, made employees feel appreciated, motivated and inspired preventing failure of small businesses.

Textural description / theme	Participants
<u>Emerging theme</u> - Failure of small businesses can be caused by poor leadership including bad decision-making, inability to lead, and reinforce business policies and not people-oriented.	3, 4, 6, 9, 10.

Textural Description: - Participant 6 said:

I believe you as owner leaders of small business need to motivate and inspire employees, make them feel they are part of the business to succeed. Otherwise, the business will fail. Rewarding employees, complementing and telling them how they and the business are doing, barbecuing and offering picnics as a form of appreciation goes a long way in preventing failure.

Participant 9 commented:

Leaders could meet regularly, hold company meetings to discuss the problems, receive employee feedback, take suggestions and opinions for the business. Communication is important. Meet on success and not at times of crisis only. Someone working for you needed motivation and inspiration to feel good and appreciated without which employees feel bad and unwanted, their efforts are unappreciated.

According to Participant 10, business was good when a leader was inspirational to workers. A leader could make employees feel that the job is important. "The worst thing is when you work in a place where you feel that your efforts are not making a difference or doing nothing" (Participant 10). Low morale results in better business failure while 126 high work morale leads to reduced production preventing failure of small businesses.The first minor theme was making a difference in production and work environment as illustrated in Tables 31.

Table 31
Failure of small businesses can be caused by inability of leader to motivate and inspire makes a difference in production and work environment

Emerging theme	Participants
Failure of small businesses can be caused by inability of leader to motivate and inspire makes a difference in production and work environment	1, 10

Textural Description: The ability of a leader to motivate and inspire makes a difference. Participant 1 said, "Leaders could motivate and inspire because it makes a difference, are part of what makes the businesses run efficiently and therefore significant."

According to Participant 10:
Business is good when a leader is inspirational to workers. A leader could make employees feel that the job is important. The worst thing is when you work in a place where you feel that your efforts are not making a differ-ence/doing nothing.

The second minor theme was allowing employees to work to the fullest or maximum capacity as illustrated in Tables 32.

Table 32
Failure of small businesses can be caused by inability of leader to motivate and inspire to allow employees work to maximum capacity

Emerging theme	Participants
Failure of small businesses can be caused by inability of leader to motivate and inspire to allow employees work to maximum capacity	1, 5

Textural Description: "Leaders could motivate and inspire because it makes a difference, are part of what makes the business run efficiently and therefore significant"

(Participant 1). Participant 5 reinforced the significance of leader's motivation and inspiration stating, "If you cannot motivate your employees they do not work to the maximum. Unmotivated workers offer inferior services, such as do not welcome customers appropriately. Motivated workers have increased morale and inspired to work to the capacity."

The focus of the originally emerging themes from Interview Questions 10 - 15 was on non-leadership factors contributing to the failure of small businesses. The reduction and elimination stages were clustered into three major themes and two minor ones. The majority of the participants commented on all non-leadership factors, such as location, size, culture, and difficulty in funding and planning. The major themes clustered included un-strategic business location, business overexpansion, low culture-based consumption, bad credit complicated ability to receive loans, and lack of budgeting and knowledge from poor planning. Minor themes clustered included inaccessible location, the culture of over-trusting, family operated with no experience, and lack of creativity, lack of capital and inability to assess business status.

When presented with Interview Question 10: "What is your perception and explanation about non-leadership factors, such as small business location, size, planning, and funding contributing to failure of small businesses?, all the participants responded positively that non-leadership factors played a major role in failure of small businesses as illustrated in Tables 33 - 38.

Table 33
Failure of small businesses can be caused by poor location, such as inaccessible, non-strategic and less populated

Textural Description	Participants
Emerging theme - *Failure of small businesses can be caused by poor location, such as inaccessible, non-strategic and less populated*	1, 5, 6, 7, 9, 10

Textural Descriptions: Some locations work or do not work well for customers. Small businesses necessitated a working location to prevent failure (Participant 1). Participant 5 said, "Location of a business is where the people can come. Small businesses fail when located in rural areas whereas the market is limited in less population." "Location is the most important thing in serving the basic business site for the targeted market or population without which the business will fail" (Participant 6).

Participant 7 commented, "Business location is significant for small business success or failure. Poor business location, such as, far from highways, poor exit and entrance for customers, and in the remote location, pose inconvenience to customers that result in small business failure. Participant 9 added:

> "If there are two to three businesses of the same product in a common location, that is a wrong location because competition may lead to failure. To prevent failure of small businesses, owner leaders could look for an area to sell the product. A socioeconomic area with less number of stores is the right place to locate the small business/area with a large number of stores is competitive and therefore a wrong place for small businesses."

Participant 10 agreed, stating:

> "The location is very important because it offers a place for business. Small business owners must find a place where there is demand for the goods and services / a leader needs to go and find a place of need. Returns are higher and businesses more successful in a more relevant area and fail in poor areas or location."

Culture-based consumption, trust, family operated, lack of versatility (same mindset) was another emerging theme as illustrated in Table 34.

Table 34

*Failure of small businesses can be caused by Culture e.g ,
trust, and family operated, lack*

Textural Description	Participants
Emerging theme - Failure of small businesses can be caused by Culture e.g. , trust, and family operated, lack	1, 3, 4, 5, 6, 9

Textural Description: Trust is a common aspect of small businesses. Participant 1 commented "A lot of People trusted with small businesses take advantage, do not have the best interest of the business. Some borrow from the business without paying back and this resulting in accumulated debts and ultimately failure of the business." Participant 3 added, "Family members inherit businesses and are obligated to operate the businesses even though with the lack of interests leading to failure. Some inherit businesses they have least experience and knowledge leading to failure."

Participant 4 commented "Lack of versatility as a culture means everything is the same, everyone has the same mindset, and this contributes to small business failure. What is needed is a new creative mindset, something new for small business to succeed." "Some people from a culture that consumes less of certain goods. Small business owners need to stock the highly traditionally or culturally consumed goods by the surrounding people. You need to sell what people are used to consuming and sometimes influenced by culture (Participant 5). Participant 6 concurred:

Small business owners need to know that culture can contribute to the failure of businesses. Involving and over-trusting family members and friends some of whom may not have business knowledge may mislead and misuse business assets resulting in failure. Culture plays a big part as some family members feel entitled. Educating and creating awareness that involving friends and family in business is a bad culture and contributes to failure is necessary. Culture needs to be monitored and scrutinized to avoid failure of small businesses.

"Most small businesses are owned by people with foreign cultures. Some cultures have bad perceptions about people coming to open businesses" (Participant 9). Funding difficulties result in the lack of Capital, loans, and bad credit was another emerging theme as illustrated in Table 35.

Table 35

Failure of small businesses can be caused by funding difficulties - result from lack of Capital, loans, and bad credit

Emerging theme	Participants
Failure of small businesses can be caused by funding difficulties - result from lack of Capital, loans, and bad credit	3, 4, 5, 6, 9, 1(

Textural Descriptions - Participant 3 said, "Reputable businesses get loans easily and contribute to the success of the business. However, bad credit makes it harder to acquire loans to start or expand leading to failure". Participant 4 commented:

> Yes, difficulties in acquiring funding affects the ability to prevent failure of small businesses. Credit scores, bad credit, type of banks that offer loans, insufficient assets

pose lending limitations. The banks that offer small businesses loans figure out what you want and when the banks learn that your credit score is low, they turn you away, then to another bank which would turn down your borrowing needs. The difficulties in borrowing contribute to small business failure. Replenishment vendors use credit worthiness, and if there are no funds, vendors cannot distribute your products resulting in failure.

Difficulty in acquiring funds results in the lack of capital need to start and establish small businesses. Small business owners struggle getting items for sale when they start small businesses with small or no amount of money (Participant 5). Banks do not offer money to owners whose small businesses do not make profits. Participant 6 said:

> You must proof to the bank that the business is generating money. Small business owners need collateral security for bank loans. These conditions are hard to meet as small business owners, complicated funding process and therefore failure of small businesses. No enough funds to finance your business results in failure. According to Participant 9, a lot of small businesses did not apply for small business loans and unless they had enough capital, failure of businesses occurred.

Some small business owners do not have sufficient money to operate businesses, such as to pay employees' salaries for six months that are necessary during business establishment. Others are poor spenders resulting in failure because there is insufficient supply, loss of sales and profits and ultimate failure. Participant 10 said, "To acquire small business loans with easy, you need to pay your bills on time and stand better chances to succeed. Late payment of bills increases difficulties in acquiring loans, and this enhances failure of small businesses." The other emerging theme was poor planning as illustrated in Table 36.

Table 36

Failure of small businesses can be caused by poor planning that results in lack of knowledge, business understanding, and business assessment

Emerging theme	Participants
Failure of small businesses can be caused by poor planning that results in lack of knowledge, business understanding, and business assessment	1, 3, 6, 9

Textural Description: - "If unaware of need, location costs of living, expenses more than income, it is because of poor planning," said Participant 1. Participant 3 concurred when commented, "Poor Planning has a big impact toward failure. You have to have a plan, try things and if the plan does not work have a backup plan, trying another even after failure. Lack of planning contributes to failure". Poor planning results from the lack of knowledge about generally targeted population, proper location, and finances to support the business (Participant 6). Participant 9 said:

> From the word go, you have to be more or less visionary, do the assessment and have a business plan. You cannot jump from one thing to another as the owner of small business. You need a plan without which business fails. Planning is necessary as it enables one know what to do

so as not to deviate from the objectives and goals. A plan allows one to assess the business to know what is working and if not, make changes or need a backup plan.

The theme of small-size resulting in limited customers and market, sales, revenue, and profits is illustrated in Table 37.

Table 37
Failure of small businesses can be caused by size as customers and market are limited, sales, revenue, and profits are small.

Textural Description	Participants
Emerging theme - *Failure of small businesses can be caused by size as customers and market are limited, sales, revenue, and profits are small.*	1, 9

Participant 1's comment about size, was:
"I think when small businesses expand it is the harder to generate more capital to fund the business. Smaller businesses are easier to control, manage, increased sales and succeed. Small businesses fail when they expand because owners do not make enough to keep them open. No enough business and chain of locations."

Participant 9 added:
You cannot go there with 5000/or a lot of people because you set up yourself for failure. Start a small business with few people able to handle different duties to serve the in-

tended clienteles. Increase the number of workers gradually as the business grows. Maintain the ideal business size to meet the demand instead of having too much supply/inventory than needed.

The originally emerging themes from Interview Questions 16 reduction and elimination stage were clustered into one main theme that contributes to the failure of small businesses. Unique features of small businesses are distinct to small businesses that inevitably result in failure of small businesses. The theme of small businesses operated with limited capital, stock, and affected adversely by the economic crisis was mentioned widely by the majority of the participants as illustrated in Table 38.

Table 38
Failure of small businesses can be caused by limited resources - capital, goods, and services and adversely affected during economic crisis

Textural description / theme	Participant
Failure of small businesses can be caused by limited resources - capital, goods, and services and adversely affected during economic crisis	1, 5, 6, 7, 10.

Textural Description: According to Participant 1, owners of small businesses started businesses with a certain budget, but when costs rose, the budget was constrained, lack capital for expansion and sales declined. "I put all my money in the business with a payoff expectation, but when the economic crisis came, I was forced to close down" (Participant 1). Participant 5 said, "Starting a small business with small and limited money hinders quick business growth. Fewer items meant low output and increased small business failure. More money means more items for sale, more profits, and business success."

Participant 6 commented:
When you operate a small business on insufficient money, then you will be in trouble during a financial crisis. In case you run into a deep hole you will be in problem during the financial crisis because no much options would be available for cushioning. Operating small business with limited resources results in failure at times of financial crisis.

Participant 7 concurred, "Yes, I believe the unique characteristic of small business owners operating on limited resources inevitably results in failure. Owners of small business need to afford materials to provide services." Participant 10 said:
You may end up with upside loans at times of financial crisis. At times of crisis, businesses do not do well, owners pay more or decide to close the business down as the returns are not worthy to keep running the business. Limited resources constrain sales, and the owners need some form of a financial cushion as the crisis worsens increasing social stress.

Structural Discussions of the Main Research Question

The participants explained the lived experiences concerning the failure of small businesses. The participants' descriptions and perceptions of the lived experiences were centered on the small business owner leaders' inabilities to institute proper leadership causing failure of small businesses. In describing the lived experiences, the participants used words such as poor leadership, planning, budgeting, lack of prior leadership skills and experiences, inability to lead, take charge and control, unable to motivate and inspire, allocate resources properly, advertise and seek for better opportunities. The words were used to place emphasis on the theme of failure of small businesses can be caused by poor or lack of leadership.

When discussing the main research question, the participants' varied descriptions centered on the how poor leadership contributed to a larger extent in the perception of failure of small businesses. All but Participant 8 concurred in many comments describing the lived experiences about the phenomenon. For example, Participant 1 said:

> Small business owner leaders perceive the failure of small businesses as a failure of leadership. If the businesses lack leadership/broken, the businesses will ultimately fail. Leaders of failed small businesses lack the ability to plan, organize and execute business functions for survival.

"Failure of small businesses result from failure of everything. However, owner leadership is the primary contributing factor. Leadership must understand the nature of a business and its operations" (Participant 2). Participant 3 concurred, "Number one is how you make people feel about doing business with you," Participant 5 said:

> "Failure of small businesses is a process. Small businesses do not fail in one day. Owner leaders of small businesses need to monitor closely the trend of small businesses to see if there is progress or failure and act accordingly to seek remedy or rectify. Leaders must lead to avoid failure."

The interview transcripts were used to support the theme that failure of small businesses can be caused by lack or poor leadership. Small businesses' struggle and eventual failure were used to emphasize the significance of owner leaders in proper business operations. In the discussions, the participants argued that bad decisions of small business owner leaders' were the main cause of failure of small businesses. Participants 1, 3, and 6 made suggestion needed to prevent failure of small businesses.

Owner leaders needed to expand the number of customers by leading employees to accomplish the mission of driving sales (Participant 4), and to allocate employees on different appropriate duties (Participant 8). Failure of small businesses can be avoided if proper leadership is put in place (Participant 7). Taking care of customers and employees is necessary (Participant 9). Motivation and rewards allow employees to be dedicated without which failure is inevitable (Participant 10). The transcripts were used to confirm that failure of small businesses can be caused by lack of leadership, motivation, and inspiration.

Composite Description

The participants' descriptions depicted that failure of small businesses was a painful and difficult learning experiences. Suggesting that diverse factors contributed to the failure of small businesses, the participants placed substantial emphasis on lack or poor leadership, limited resources, knowledge, and planning. Many participants' suggested that failure of small businesses happened because operating a successful business required substantial leadership abilities, such as proper planning, good leadership styles, and decision-making, motivating, inspiring, communication, trust, and vision. Most of the small business owner leaders lacked the identified leadership traits that resulted in failure. The general difficulties encountered by the participants included optimism in descriptions about the future impending business endeavors, problems with the leadership, the reputation of small businesses, location, and sustainability.

Summary

Chapter 4 was a presentation of the findings from interviewing the participants as owner leaders of small businesses who experienced failure of small businesses. The participants described lived experiences concerning the phenomenon and the predominant causes. The discussion documentation in Chapter 4 included the process used in selecting and locating the participants and conducting actual interviews.

Moreover, precautions were taken to ensure the protection of the participants' rights and privacy.

Included in Chapter 4 were the seven step procedures of Van Kaam modified approach that allow a deeper insight of the studied phenomenon (Moustakas, 1994). The procedure of van Kaam modified approach was used to abstract the owner leaders' expressions for analysis as used to describe the lived experiences from interview transcripts. Analyzing the expressions resulted in emerging of nine themes about causes of failure of small businesses. The themes were used to identify the causes of failure of small businesses including poor leadership, limited resources, knowledge, and planning.

Chapter 5 is a presentation of recommendations and conclusions of the study. The chapter is not only intended to present but also interpret drawn conclusions from the study findings of the collected data. Included in the chapter is the discussion of study findings and conclusions arrived; significance of the findings and implications and future research recommendations for the failure of small businesses.

Chapter 5
Conclusions and Recommendations

■ The application of funding options to the business from personal revenues means that measures could be taken to limit liabilities to the business without extending the losses to personal capital or assets.

The purpose of the qualitative phenomenological intrinsic study was to explore the lived experiences of small business owner leaders who experienced failure of small businesses. The method of data collection included a purposive sample of the participants who agreed voluntarily to participate in the study. The selected participants for the research held lived experiences concerning the failure of small businesses.

Public records maintained by the city of San Jose, California were used to identify and locate owner leaders of small businesses to participate in the interviews. Failure in the study represented the termination of the business operations to avoid bankruptcy or further financial losses (Headd, 2003). Furthermore, interest was specifically focused on the failure of small businesses for small businesses.

Review of the Research Study

Chapter 5 consisted of three main parts. Part 1 is a presentation of a broad discussion and a review of Chapters 1, 2, and 3, which entailed the understanding of the problem and purpose of the study. Part 2 was used to provide a discussion and implications of the findings of the study as presented in Chapter 4. Part 3 is the main basis of Chapter 5, a presentation of the study's recommendations and conclusions.

Part I:
Understanding the Problem and the
Study's Purpose

Chapter 1 contained a discussion of the problem of the failure of small businesses and the study's purpose of exploring the failure of the small business phenomenon. The presentation of the discussions was used to define the significance of small businesses to the economy of the United States and the effect of increasing failure rates.

Understanding the failure of small businesses phenomenon was attained by interviewing direct experiences of owner leaders who experienced failure. The insight is significant for organizational leaders in the policy-making process.

Review of the Significance of the Study to Research and Leadership

A review of prior literature used to examine the failure of small businesses did not result in a predominant cause (Rogoff et al., 2004) of failure of small businesses. The current study's findings resulted in increased knowledge as was used to offer a deeper understanding of the phenomenon of failure of small businesses. The study's information gained may be used as a foundation for leaders in making decisions.

Leaders can make use of the new sources of information concerning the failure of small businesses. Bass (1990) argued that the ability of leaders in making informed decisions was significant in any organization advocating for a need for reliable information. Interpretation of the study's importance recognized the development of informational source that reduced the uncertainties when taking into account what causes failure of small businesses.

Interpreting the Literature Review

The approach in Chapter 2 was general to specific mainly to enhance the phenomenon's understanding. Emphasis was placed on understanding the meaning of failure of small businesses by definitions and the historical development from the origin. Chapter 2 discussions were used to reiterate the fact that a predominant cause for the failure of small businesses was yet to be identified (Maes et al., 2005; Rogoff et al., 2004). Exponents of the prior theories offered numerous causes for failure of small businesses (Beaver, 2003; Stanford, 1982), and therefore offered organizational leaders with an unclear understanding of the causes. The revelation from the literature review was that there existed a need for further research to attain a greater insight of the causes of failure of small businesses.

Explaining the Research Methodology and Design

Chapter 3 was used to present the qualitative research methodology and the appropriateness of the design. The qualitative methodology was necessarily appropriate in understanding the phenomenon of failure of small businesses because it allowed a focused consideration in understanding the present problem in entirety (Vishnevsky & Beanlands, 2004). Researchers used a qualitative methodology to gain broad and unique insight of a phenomenon (Creswell, 2002).

The research was integrated into van Kaam modified approach and a phenomenological design to attain an understanding of the failure of small businesses. The approach applied was focused on attaining a clear and non-biased result (Blum & Muirhead, 2005; Moustakas, 1994). The researcher used personal interviews to obtain lived experiences of every small business owner-leader who participated.

Interpreting the Data Analysis

Chapter 4 was a presentation of the current study's findings. Included in the chapter was the process of data gathering and the approach applied in the data analysis. Data interpretation resulted in the generation of themes used to describe small businesses owner leaders' lived experiences as associated to the failure of small businesses.

Part II:
Implications of Study's Findings

The results of the findings in the current study are aligned with previous research (Byrne, 2009). The general areas of alignment consisted of factors contributing to the failure of small businesses, such as poor leadership, limited resources, lack of business knowledge and planning. The implication of the study's findings was a fascinating nuance for small businesses as it associated the distinctiveness of leadership to the enterprises (Rogoff, et al., 2004).

Leadership, as associated with leading employees, is not relevant always to small business enterprises (Maryland Chamber of Commerce, 2004). Harold et al., (2011) agreed that in most cases, small business enterprises are sole owner operated with few or no more employees. In such cases, small business owner leaders do not have anybody as followers or to lead.

Discussion of Themes

Every research participant responded to 16 interview questions out of three broader sub-research questions that were used to focus on three main areas: i) unique small business characteristics, ii) leadership, and iii) non-leadership areas. The recording, transcribing and analyzing of the participants' responses ensued. A review of the participants' responses disclosed a widespread pattern about the phenomenon of failure of small businesses. The following nine major themes emerged from the review of the participants' responses describing the lived experiences concerning the failure of small businesses;

1. Lack of funding, limited resources, and funding difficulties.
2. Failure of small businesses can be caused by lack of knowledge and understanding.
3. Failure of small businesses can be caused by poor leadership involving not people-oriented, poor business operations, closed most days, lack of trust, communication and customer service.
4. Economic crisis including underdevelopment of the economy.
5. poor business location such as un-strategic and low populated areas can result in failure of small businesses.
6. Lack of motivation and inspiration can cause failure of small businesses.
7. Culture - some goods are lowly consumed based on the culture of the people in the community.
8. Size - Expansion of small businesses results in funding difficulties.
9. Poor Planning results in a lack of business understanding and knowledge, and Improper business assessment.

(1)Lack of funding, limited resources, and funding difficulties. Participant 2 commented, "Small business owners lack sufficient resources to use in operating businesses because capital is drawn from personal income. During dip cycles in economic performances and lack of customers, businesses come second in preference resulting to small business failure." Participant 1 said:

> Yes, you start a business with a certain budget, but when costs rise, budget is constrained, no income for expansion, and sales decline. I put all my money in the business with a payoff expectation, but when the economic crisis came, I was forced to close down.

"Unlike large businesses with stakeholders, small business owners are the only self-partners of the businesses that cause capital limitation and failure of the business" (Participant 5).

The inability to fund a business can cause failure because the lack of funds affected the general business performance (Gregory et al., 2005). Problems associated with acquiring funds cause limitations to owner leaders' performing abilities. The owner leaders are thrown into a quagmire that complicates failure preventing efforts. Cressy (2006) believed that availability of sufficient funds enhanced small business owner leaders' abilities to generate more finances required for the businesses. Most owner-leaders financed small businesses from limited private funds (Lappalainen & Niskanen, 2013) and per most participants' suggestions, small business leader owners fund businesses from limited personal or individual savings.

The owner leaders of small businesses do not attain stability when funding businesses through personal savings because of increased personal or individual risks associated with the business endeavor. Drawing personal or individual insufficient resources limit the small business enterprising activities. A review of the previous studies revealed that small business owner leaders possessed limited resources to finance the business during difficult economic times compared to large businesses (Dawley et al., 2003), impeding the ability to prevent failure. Small business owner leaders have the capacity to generate a flow of funds or even establish a strong customer-based environment to aid business operations. Failure of small businesses happens when the capacities are ignored to sustain the businesses.

The participants of the present study supported Cressy's (2006) findings that failure of small businesses was most likely to occur in first two years. Small business ownership possesses arbitrary limitations, such as lack of resources to start and affecting business operation, capacity to generate profits, sustain and develop the business. Owner leaders of small businesses can meet only the customers' needs aligned with what the business is capable of manufacturing.

Small business owner leaders have no option but manage all the operations given that employees are minimal or none. Capacities of owner leaders to generate profits or cash-flow are significant in preventing failure when private funding is difficult. Thornhill and Amit (2003) concurred when asserted that failure of small businesses happens commonly at earlier developmental stages of an organization when business is small and leaders are not well experienced.

(2). Failure of small businesses can be caused by lack of knowledge and understanding. Lack of leaders' knowledge contributes to the failure of small businesses (Audretsch, 2012). Bouchikhi (1993) agreed that technical knowledge or skills are not the same as the knowledge necessary in leading or operating a business. Unknowledgeable about producing goods and services can contribute to the failure of small businesses. Participant 1 said, "Lack of knowledge can inevitably contribute to the failure of small businesses. When people hired in small business know that the owner is not aware, they take advantage and eventually run-down the business."

Participant 2 said, " A lack of knowledge may result in the lack of understanding about small business funding and other factors such as government regulations, pricing and branding that ultimately affect small businesses adversely. Small business owners' lack of understanding may result in failure."

"Lack of knowledge has a lot of impacts. One needs to know the product, where to sell it, at least area code, accommodating customers instead of saying I don't know" (Participant 3). Participant 4 said, "I took businesses classes where I learned about business plans, marketing, and areas needed to establish a business."

Participant 5 commented, "Most leaders do not have the knowledge of handling the business. The owner-leaders of small businesses need to understand how to manage the business. You can manage a business without knowing you are making losses until business collapses."

Carter and Van Auken (2006) argued that lack or shortage of knowledge, such as imperfect market pricing for goods and services in an industry may impact the capacity to generate profits or necessary cash-flow that results in failure. Owner leaders' knowledge about adequate pricing was significantly used in preventing failure of businesses. Superior data, information, and knowledge were used to produce an adequate business decisions and business action plans (Frey, 2001).

(3). Failure of small businesses can be caused by poor leadership such as not people-oriented, poor business operations, closed most days, lack of trust, communication, and customer service. Participant 5 said,

> "Failure of small businesses results from poor leadership style and lack of vision, lack of prior leadership experiences, poor employee management and unable to take employees' constructive feedback, no plan of action, do not market the business product, unable to work with employees and customers, does not follow through, lacks business knowledge, ineffective resource allocation, bad business decisions, lacks communication and untrustworthy."

Failures of small businesses occur when leaders lack experiences in leadership.Participant 1 said:

> Small business owners perceive the failure of small businesses as a failure of leadership. If the businesses lack leadership/broken, the businesses will ultimately fail. Leaders of failed small businesses lack the ability to plan,

organize and execute business functions for survival. Most owners of small businesses have not held leadership positions and starting to lead people will be a little harder because of the owners' views about what constitutes proper leadership.

Successful small business owner leaders are educated, trained and hold prior hands-on skills in leadership. "There is a need for business leaders to be educated through the bachelor's degree" (Participant 4).

Participant 9 commented,

> "First, if a person is not trained or has not worked in a small business environment, failure may occur. This is because the person may lack leadership skills, not know how to talk to people, train employees, meet and greet clienteles. According to Participant 10, "Leadership is very significant as the failure of businesses occurs when proper leadership lacks. Good leadership results in good businesses because good leaders lead businesses well."

Participant 8 said:

"Poor leaders are unfair, uncompromising and not ready to take opinions, suggestions of employees and customers seriously leading to failure of small businesses. A person may lack leadership skills, not know how to talk to people, train employees, meet and greet clienteles. Also, some leaders want to be authoritarian and look down upon employees, and this contributes to the failure of small businesses. Good leadership is to expand the number of customers by leading employees to accomplish the mission of driving sales, allocate employees on different duties. Poor leaders do not take efforts in advertising and promoting the marketing of products."

Preventing failure of small businesses needs a leader who is knowledgeable about what is happening around the business, follow through and stick to it. Participant 4 said, "I was not really hustling to succeed, and therefore failure come along." Most leaders do not have the knowledge of handling the business leading to failure. Owner leaders of small businesses need to understand how to manage the business.

Participant 5 agreed that "You can manage a business without knowing you are making losses until business collapses." Participant 10 added, "Yes, no failures may occur with good leaders. A leader has to be the captain of the ship. A leader needs to know all the business departments, what business other people are doing and even the failing departments."

Like in any businesses, poor leadership results in bad business decisions, such as, misuse of business financial reserves that leads to the struggle for business success and ultimate failure (Participant 2). Participant 2 continued:
>Lack of leadership is more of a major problem with small than large businesses that contribute to failure, and therefore small businesses require more leadership involvement. Failure of small businesses happens when no one seems to be accountable, responsible and in full control as a leader.

Participant 3 said, "Being honest and trustworthy as leaders, personable, polite, knowledgeable, personality, presentable, and caring about customers and businesses impact the leader's capacity to prevent failure." Participant 4 added: Successful leaders are proactive, surrounded with the right people; go out to acquire information that contributes toward the success of a small business to prevent failure. I perceive leadership as important because there has to be a leader well informed to hold everything together. Otherwise, everything breaks down resulting in failure.

Participant 6 commented:
A business that lacks proper leadership will not get off the ground. Lack of leadership would enable other competitors to take over the market share and ground your business that results in failure. A leader has to communicate the business' mission to employees adequately. A leader must be able to work with employees and customers, trusted to fulfill the promises, advice in advance if not going to fulfill the promises to prevent failure.

What you need to know is the future of the business and how to project. According to Participant 5:
As owner-leader of a small business, you need to stop and reevaluate to see what is going well and not look for measures when you realize things are not going well (visionary). Do not wait till there is huge deep or losses to make changes. Lack of vision and failure to analyze and evaluate the business early enough results to failure.

Participant 7 commented that "Good leadership means staying on budget. Poor leadership overstretches the business budget from over-recruiting employees, not assigning employees to specific and ideal jobs, leads to confusion, and lack of understanding of roles and duties and eventually failure of businesses." Moreover, Participant 8 added, "my product as a traveling agency was unique that depended largely on leadership style for success or failure." A leadership style is used to determines how business is run, and poor leadership can adversely impact small businesses. A leader can learn new ways of adapting and adjusting to different leadership styles to prevent failure of small businesses (Participant 8).

Prior researchers viewed poor leadership as shortfalls and underperformance in leadership (Chavan, 2005; Evans, 2005; Harris & Gibson, 2006; Harris, Grubb, & Hebert, 2005; McCartan-Quinn & Carson, 2003), which notably contributed to the failure of small businesses. The underperforming and shortfall displayed by leaders reflect the inability to generate suitable cultures within organizations needed in preventing failure (Campbell, 2004; Chen, 2004; Schein, 2004). The shortfalls are also obstacles for leaders to adapt successfully to changing business environment (Handy & Levis, 2001). The decision-making process is centered on many factors (Greenberg & Lowrie, 2012; Kurtz & Snowden, 2003; Senior & Copley, 2008).

Shaw (2007) argued that leadership process necessitated influence either in a group context or setting that involved goal accomplishment that reflected a shared vision. A broad review of theoretical frameworks about competent leadership showed that previous leadership theories were focused on leaders' characteristics while the most recent ones were used to emphasize the relative factors that impacted leadership including followers' role (Gosling, Martuano, & Dennison, 2003). Proper leadership supports organizational strategies by encouraging stability of an organization, high morale of employees, engagement, and advocate for stable funding via continuity of the business (Collins, 2009; Garman & Tyler, 2007). The managerial strategy of a talented individual varies from one organization to another depending on the organization's styles of leadership and culture (Jackson & Watson, 2009) lead to failure.

Hammond, Keeney, and Raiffa (1999) associated rational decision-making process with elements such as identifying the problem, aims and objectives, options, uncertainties, risk-taking, tradeoffs, and other decisions linked to good leadership. Krogerus and Tschäppeler (2008) concurred with the argument that decision-making process encompassed situation deconstruction system during chaotic periods to expose action-based elements. Decision-makers attained widespread overview as the situations were simplified. Failure is the complexity of the situation as a problem. Properly defining the problem gives owner leaders a broader problem overview that allows prevention alternatives.

Small business owner leaders need to display a high degree of disciplined focus and commitment as lack the attributes result in failure (Gaskill et al., 1993). Gaskill et al. (1993) argued that failure or success of business resulted from non-leadership causes that enhanced employees' motivation to accomplish tasks. Small business owner leaders employ themselves without direct supervisors and external motivation. Training and education also are significant in leadership positions as leaders generate and develop a plan of action to prevent failure of small businesses (Cobley, 2015).

Communication involves the dissemination of ideas, thoughts, attitudes and feelings from one place to another via the medium (Sangeetha, 2012). The barriers to communication are obstacles to clear understanding of problems. Ineffective communication results in distortion, alteration leading to anxiety, poor priorities, anger, and unfocused vision (United States Coast Guard, 1998). Morale is lower with ineffective communication, and that results in failure of businesses. Effective communication allows employees to build healthy relationships used to avoid failure of small businesses.

Poor leadership was not only noted as significant in contributing to the failure of small businesses, but the theme was also the basis for describing how leadership performed a unique function of owners of small businesses. Small business enterprises are sometimes operated by a sole employee who is the owner-leader without a need for followers to lead. Limited resources such as funding difficulties pose limitations for small business growth and the option of keeping or hiring workers.

(4). Economic crisis including underdevelopment of the economy. Participant 8 responded that "I agree that increasing failure rates hurt small business owner and stuff as large businesses are buying out small business leadership and employees. The transitions to new positions hurt small businesses and the economy as a whole." Participant 3 said:,

I believe increasing failure rate trend of small businesses has a great impact on the economy. I believe people feel more comfortable dealing with small businesses than large businesses. Failure of small businesses tears communities a part. Closing down of small businesses tear down communities as a result of lack of products close to the people.

Participant 5 commented, "Increasing failure rate trend is killing the economy. When small businesses are failing in mass level, people do not pay taxes and the government lacks the money needed for development and public service." "Small businesses contribute a lot to the growth of an economy. People lose jobs, and others may not get jobs when small businesses fail" (Participant 7). Participant 10 added, "Increasing failure rates results in no enough money to rotate back to the system. More lucrative businesses promote the economy, but failing businesses hurt the economy."

According to the U.S. Census Bureau (2014), the primary significance of small businesses included the growth of US economies. Vieira (2014) argued that small businesses' risks involved high sensitivity to the adverse economic environment. Despite the primary function of small businesses in generating employment opportunities and household incomes (Harold, Gurpreet, & Sajid, 2011), small businesses continued to fail at the rate of 50% before the fifth anniversary (Cronin-Gilmore, 2012, p. 96), which continues to hurt the economy.

(5). A poor business location such as un-strategic and low populated areas can result in failure of small businesses. Location can contribute toward small business failure. An organization's location is significant because it is used to determine the customers' accessibility depending on the nature of the business. "First, in a business community like corporate businesses, streets lead more people to the businesses. Second, In populated small towns, there is low business from the locals, and this leads to failure of small businesses in that region" commented Participant 4.

However, the advent of online technology is continuously changing the location's impact and role on the failure of small businesses. Various participants suggested that internet and websites have become important business platforms affirming Wyse's (2004) study findings. Participant 8 said:

> As a travel agency, my business failed because reaching customers in the face of the internet, website, and new technology continued to be a struggle. I used the traditional phone call to reach customers that would not successfully compete with companies that used computer technology.

A review of the previous research (Adam & Sykes, 2003; Beaver & Jennings, 2005; Gorman, 2003; Jensen & Pompelli, 2002; Pena, 2002; Shields, 2005), was used to reveal that poor business location resulted in the failure of small businesses. The current study's findings are consistent with prior research. Gupta and Govindarajan (2004) argued that though the physical business location caused impact, the influence of websites and internet on shaping and completing transactions needed to be considered. Concurring with Gupta and Govindarajan (2004), most small businesses owner leaders have replaced the features of physical boundaries with the use of the Internet and online selling.

(6). Lack of motivation and inspiration can cause failure of small businesses. Lack of motivation and inspiration results in the failure of small businesses. Inspiring and motivating employees are significant in an attempt to prevent failure (Participant 8).

Participant 5 said, "If you cannot motivate your employees will not work to the maximum. Unmotivated workers offer inferior services, such as do not welcome customers appropriately. Motivated workers have increased morale and inspired to work to the capacity."

Participant 4 said, "A leader who is more receptive to employees, follow up on employees' feedback, interaction with the employee would motivate and inspire employees to work harder and prevent failure of small businesses." Participant 10 commented:

> Business is good when a leader is inspirational to workers. A leader could make employees feel that the job is important. The worst thing is when you work in a place where you feel that your efforts are not making a difference/doing nothing. High morale results in better business while low work morale leads to low production resulting in failure.

In the present study, most of the participants described the lived experiences about motivation and inspiration, which concurred with the previous scholars. Leaders' shortfalls and underperformance include the leaders' inabilities to motivate and inspire followers to accomplish expected duties and tasks (Visser et al., 2005). Follower motivation to produce to capacity was an alignment with studies used to discuss the significance of transformational style of leadership (O'Regan & Ghobadian, 2004; Temtime & Pansiri, 2005; Visser et al., 2005). Bass (1990) argued that transformational leadership style was important in inspiring workers to perform to maximum capacity. Participant 6 said:

> I believe you as owner leaders of small business need to motivate and inspire employees, make them feel they are part of the business to succeed. Otherwise, the business will fail. Rewarding employees, complementing and telling them how they and the business are doing, barbecuing and offering picnics as a form of appreciation goes a long way in preventing failure.

Phipps, Prieto, and Verma (2012) argued for the significance of motivation and inspiration in ever-changing business environments. Motivation and inspiration resulted in better employee relationships, hard work and better response to business challenges (Joshi, Lazarova, & Liao, 2009). Gaan and Bhoon (2012) concurred by associating proper leadership to the ability to motivate and inspire enhancing workers' dedication and ultimately preventing failure.

(7). Culture - some goods are slowly consumed based on the culture of the people in the community. According to Participant 3, "Family members inherit businesses and are obligated to operate the businesses even though with the lack of interests leading to failure. Some inherit businesses they have least experience and knowledge leading to failure." Participant 1 said:

> Trust is common to small businesses. A lot of people trusted with small businesses take advantage, do not have

the best interest of the business. Some borrow from the business without paying back and this resulting in accumulated debts and ultimately failure of the business.

Participant 4 commented, "Lack of versatility as a culture means everything is the same, everyone has the same mindset, and this contributes to small business failure. What is needed is a new creative mindset, something new for small business to succeed." Participant 5 said:

> Some people from some culture consume more of certain products and less of other goods. Small business owners need to stock more of the culturally consumed by the surrounding people. You need to sell what people are used to consuming and sometimes influenced by culture.

Small business owners need to know that culture can contribute to the failure of businesses. According to Participant 6:

> Involving and over-trusting family members and friends, some of whom may not have business knowledge, may mislead and misuse business assets resulting in failure. Culture plays a big part as some family members feel entitled. Educating and creating awareness that involving friends and family in business is a bad culture and contributes to failure is necessary. Culture needs to be monitored and scrutinized to avoid failure of small businesses.

Gaskill et al. (1993) argued that the culture of employing friends and involving family members who are inexperienced and unknowledgeable to operate small businesses caused failure. The family members and friends involved do not do a good job in preventing failure because the members lack managerial competence and the necessary experiences

(Gaskill et al., 1993). Small business employees and customers bring individual experiences, norms and beliefs that help in shaping relationships in the small businesses (Madurapperuma, 2011). Madurapperuma (2011) argued that some of the social, institutional, and cultural aspects of small businesses might be good but bad ones were attributed to the failure of small businesses. Bad social aspects, such as illegal or low consumption based on culture and religion may impact the structure, formation, and operations of small business that result in failure.

(8). Size - Expansion of small businesses results in funding difficulties. Participant 1 said, "I think when small businesses expand it is the harder to generate more capital to fund the business." Because of the small-sized nature of small businesses, everything is too small compared to large businesses. Items going out are too few, less total revenue and less profit (Participant 5). Participant 6 mentioned that "Size refers to the number of customers. Smaller businesses have a smaller number of customers to compete successfully with big businesses."

Participant 10 commented about the size that, "Smaller businesses result in smaller returns, a reason why people decide to expand their businesses to increase clienteles and returns. Smaller business size results in failure." Participant 7 concurred, stating:

> Size limits the growth of small businesses. As a small business owner, I was limited to 14 kids by the state. The limitation imposed on the number of clients necessitated me operating the business with limited income and finances that resulted in failure.

Watson and Everett (1996) argued that the probability of a business to fail was higher when a business is small than large Failure rates are unimaginably higher as the size of a business decreases than when expanding. The business performance is definitely impacted by many aspects such as ownership, industry type, the level of debts, external consultancy, and most importantly, size. Perry (2001) asserted that though planning contributed to the failure of small businesses, business size played a major role in hindering effective managerial activities that resulted in failure. Concerning the key role of leading workers, successful leadership is dependent upon the business size and type.

(9). Poor Planning results in the lack of business understanding and knowledge and improper business assessment. If the owner of a small business is unaware of the business needs, location, costs of living, expenses exceeding income, it is because of poor planning (Participant 1). Participant 3 commented, "Poor Planning has a significant impact toward failure. You have to have a plan, try things and if they do not work, have a backup plan, trying another even after failure. Lack of planning contributes to failure." Participant 4 said:

Poor planning of small business owners inevitably leads to failure. Without planning as a small business owner, you are a step behind. Organized environment eases backup things in business. It is hard to catch up and get ahead when small businesses lack planning. One hundred percent planning would get you there.

Participant 10 said, "Poor Planning is number one of all. You must have a plan, such as for acquiring loans, hiring employees, what to look for in an employee, background checks, and what risks taking."

According to Participant 9:
"Poor planning - from the word go, you have to be more or less a visionary, do an assessment and draw the business plan. You cannot jump from one thing to another, need a plan without which business fails. Planning is necessary as it enables one know what to do so as not to deviate from the plan. A plan allows one to assess the business to know what is working and if not, make changes or need a backup plan."

Planning is significant for small business owner leaders to prevent failure to attain success (Ibrahim et al., 2004; Yusuf & Saffu, 2005). The present study's findings aligned with the literature review emphasizing planning necessity for increased organizational success (Ibrahim et al., 2004). Most small business owner leaders who experienced failure did not consider planning as significant before they ventured into small business enterprising. Planning and leadership contribute to organization's sustainability and continuity of the business by placing the right employees in the right positions and time performing right duties to achieve the right outcomes (Rothwell, 2010).

Part III:
Recommendations

The analysis of the lived experiences of the ten owner-leaders of small businesses who experienced failure and the themes that emerged were used to guide the study's recommendations. The following two areas are emphasized to minimize failure of small businesses (a) planning and (b) implementation. The conclusions were aligned with the literature used to identify planning as the significant factor in small businesses' success (Ibrahim et al., 2004; Yusuf & Saffu, 2005). Moreover, addressed are the arguments of the study's findings that poor or lack of planning can contribute to the failure of small businesses. Dividing planning into phases was recommended, each with an independent purpose to indicate the significance of every phase identified.

Planning Phase

In the planning phase, potential small business owner leaders could attain necessary knowledge about the businesses intended to initiate. The knowledge could not only exceed mere technical skills or knowledge but also explore into understanding the distinctiveness of the intended small businesses to operate the business effectively or become an efficient businessperson. Prior discussions about the topical and finding literature of the present study was used to suggest that one of the causes of failure of small businesses was small business owner leaders' lack of the business knowledge (Carter & Van Auken, 2006).

Extra work experience was recognized as significant when addressing the findings associated with the owner leaders' lack of knowledge. The recommendation is that at the planning phase, potential small business owner leaders could consider volunteering to work with the owner-leaders operating similar businesses. Working closely with small business owner-leaders in the same business can offer distinctive insight about the planned enterprise that can surpass mere technical skills one may hold. The researcher used the phase of planning to emphasize the issues related to the many themes recognized in the research including; lack of funding and limited resources, lack of knowledge and understanding, poor leadership, economic crisis, poor business location, lack of motivation and inspiration, culture, size, and poor planning. The phase of planning is divided into three sections.

One of the recommendations is that small business owner-leaders could undergo training to gain skills in accomplishing small businesses' mission statement, vision, and goals. Owner-leaders of small businesses could embrace efficient communication to enhance precision, concise, expedience, and intuitive behaviors at all levels of the small businesses. Proper dialogue and communication prevent failure of small businesses through improved sustainability dynamics in employee working relationships and perceptions (Beck, Bruderl, & Woywode, 2008).

It is recommended that the potential small business owner-leaders either review extensively or analyze the available funding options for the intended enterprise. Difficulties in funding posed organizational limitation for the performance capabilities and success (Gregory et al., 2005), a theme that recurred persistently during interviews with the study's participants. The situation was complicated by owner leaders' limitation to capital accessibility (Cressy, 2006). Moreover, the complexity was intensified when private lenders perceived the enterprises as riskier ventures.

In the event of unavailable private lending banks, small business owner-leaders could consider using personal resources to fund the businesses. Personal resources are not necessarily limited to the personal account but open to soliciting extra funds from friends and family members willing to assist funding. When using personal incomes to finance businesses, owner leaders need to have the knowledge and understand of the liabilities involved such as risks at the personal level as related to the financing. The application of funding options to the business from personal revenues means that measures could be taken to limit liabilities to the business without extending the losses to personal capital or assets.

Potential small business owner leaders could recognize investors willing to take risks usually avoided by banks. Investors from private sectors can provide short-term funding to enable owner-leaders of small businesses to start and establish. With every option per the participant's suggestions, potential owner leaders could verify the regular funding needs and dedicate a minimum of half year's savings before commencing business. Owner leaders of small businesses could use the savings of 6 months to survive through hard times experienced during hard economic times, a theme identified in the study.

Furthermore, the potential small business owners need to establish strong customer foundation before commencing businesses, recognize the potential loyal customer, generate dependable cash or revenue flow before launching the enterprise. The recommendation was particularly used to address themes of lack of customer services, and funding may cause failure of small businesses. Part of the recommendations was conducted complete market research before venturing into the business.

Potential and current small business owners could conduct strategic planning in a resilient manner to carry out or implement failure prevention measures. The Poor location was another theme revealed and emphasized in the study's findings as the factor contributing to the failure of small businesses. When tackling the finding, it was necessitated that owner leaders of small businesses held an insight of the market intended as associated with proper pricing, advertising needs, site as well as if the demand existed for goods and services for proper planning

Another recommendation is ensuring proper leadership in the phase of planning to address the theme of poor or lack of leadership. Shortfalls in leadership (Chavan, 2005; Evans, 2005; Harris & Gibson, 2006; Harris et al., 2005; McCartan-Quinn & Carson, 2003) were known to cause failure of small businesses. The theme was also recognized by the majority of the participants in the current study. Commenting on the study's findings, potential small business owner leaders could conduct skills assessment in an honest manner to establish whether they held skills required to the sole proprietorship and whether there is the need for help. An honest appraisal or assessment could be used to establish whether small business owner leaders meet the standards of operating small businesses such as motivating and inspiring, a theme that was realized in the study's findings.

Moreover, the current and potential small business owners could conduct exploratory research on small businesses to gain necessary knowledge for superior decision-making capacities. Small business owners could understand the formulation of managing the businesses, employees, and businesses resources, such as assets and consumer trends. The measures will be vital for potential and current small business owners to avoid failure of small businesses.

The current and potential owners of small businesses could involve in facilitating workshops to address the theme of lack of knowledge mentioned widely by the participants. The federal and state personnel in charge of administering small businesses could develop programs in leadership to evaluate and assist owner leaders of small businesses in transitioning of leadership traits required for the success of small businesses past five years of operation. In the workshops, the small business owners could work in collaboration with officers of Small Business Association (SBA) and the incubators from the neighborhood, who provide many years of accumulated experiences as most successful small business owners.

Both current and potential small business owners would gain from different research findings and knowledge disseminated in the workshops. The benefits for the owners of small businesses may include; managing the decision-making strategies and practices to avoid failure of small businesses. Furthermore, current and potential small business owners could monitor the trends on a regular basis and projected business speculation and optimism is often a good direction.

In overcoming the theme of hard economic crisis contributing to failure, small business owners could research in respective industries and exercise diligence prior commencing the businesses to develop the insight about the market demand and supply, competitors, and general market saturation. Moreover, the owners of small businesses could provide the government agencies with the correct information and data to enhance the understanding of perceptions of the small business owners who experienced failure for better support. Governments could formulate policies that help in sustaining of small businesses during an economic crisis

Furthermore, the current and potential small business owners could accumulate capital to overcome the theme of small size contributing to the failure of small businesses as identified by most participants. Mueller and Stegmaier (2015) argued that the small-size nature of the businesses is a liability to small businesses. Shocks experienced randomly cause the demise of small businesses but are unnoticed in large businesses. Small businesses characterized by little capital for an organization are riskier to fail. Owners of small businesses with plenty capital enable small businesses to survive numerous adverse economic shocks. Unlike small businesses, large businesses with large capital enjoy economies of large scale, exercise diversification and easily spread business risks across many shareholders strengthening the economic base (Carreira and Silva 2010). Larger businesses command stronger market share and sway government decisions and show little failure risks.

Implementation

In the ending phase of implementation, owner leaders of small businesses could concentrate around self-rational outlook. As evident in the study's themes and findings unrealistic decision-making impacts the success of owner leaders of small businesses. To tackle the finding will necessitate owner leaders of small businesses to align adequately rational thinking with making realistic decisions.

Future owner leaders of small businesses could foresee facing challenges and ready to survive during harder economic times usually common in the developmental stage of small businesses. The suggestion was held by the study's findings that failure of small businesses is predominant at earlier developmental stages of businesses (Thornhill & Amit, 2003). Owners of small businesses could get ready to face competition and understand that competing favorably needed advertisement. The recommendation is tailored by the findings used to advocate the idea that small businesses lack advertisement compared to larger businesses.

Limitations and Future Research

Many areas do exist for future research to take consideration. The limitation experienced in the current study comprised of scope, resources and time. Narrowing the scope, the focus was only on failure of small businesses in San Jose, California and excluded other cities or states excluded. Furthermore, the focus was not only used to exclude any other cities and states but posed limitation of the sample population concerning the category of participants. There was also a limitation regarding the study's purpose to understand the meaning of the lived experiences of the phenomenon and not the success.

Narrowing the study to the present level of detail was used to help complete the research within the course time frame but limited likelihood to attain a broader understanding of factors that cause failure of small businesses. A limitation emerged in assumptions that small business owner leaders' goal was to generate profit and prevent failure. A surmounting number of owner leaders of small businesses interested in gaining experiences only in the enterprises while ignoring the likelihood of failure hindered the ability of the researcher to gain a deeper understanding of the causes of failure of small businesses. Gaining a broader insight of the phenomenon was limited as the concentration was only on particular goals of owner leaders of small businesses, such as preventing failure and profit making.

Future research concentrating on the failure of small businesses could conquer the limitations because a need exists to understand the failure of small businesses from a wider perspective. Elimination of the constraints of time may allow an examination to understand how failure phenomenon is uniquely distributed across the cities or states. Studies comparing results among or between various cities or states may offer valuable insight of how the causes compare in different cities or states.

Future research studies could include a reflection on a more different sample population and put emphasis on aspects, such as gender, age, or size of small businesses. The research could be used to explore the connection between the variables and participants' lived experiences concerning causes of failure of small businesses. There exists a need to comprehend lived experiences of small business owner leaders who succeeded and the measures taken to prevent failure.

Lastly, an improved insight of failure could be achieved if a study was performed using a different meaning of failure. The meaning applied in the current study did not include closures and separated financially distressed organizations. A study's result integrating closures when defining failure and imitating the researcher's approach could offer comparisons to a different view of the problem.

Summary

The purpose of the qualitative phenomenological intrinsic study was to explore the lived experiences of small business owner leaders who experienced failure of small. Chapter 5 entailed a presentation of a review of the prior chapters pursued by the discussion of the study's findings and inferences. The nine themes realized as probable causes of small business failure included; (a) lack of funding, limited resources, and funding difficulties including; (b) lack of knowledge and understanding; (c) poor leadership involving not people-oriented, poor business operations, closed most days, lack of trust, communication and customer service; (d) economic crisis including underdevelopment of the economy; (e) poor business location such as un-strategic and low populated areas can result in failure of small businesses; (f) lack of motivation and inspiration; (g) culture; (h) size; and (i) poor planning.

Included was the discussion of the study's limitations and suggestions for the future research. The focus of the present study was to comprehend the lived experiences of owner leaders of small businesses who experienced failure instead of success. The conclusion in Chapter 5 included a presentation of viable recommendations to avoid failure of small businesses in future, which is, in two phases identified (a) planning and (b) implementation. The recommendations were tailored on each of the nine themes used to identify the causes of failure of small businesses. Particular focus was not only on poor leadership but also poor planning prior commencing business, generating funding options, and conducting an honest assessment of leadership capabilities.

Reflections on the Progress of the Research Experience

The qualitative phenomenological intrinsic research was used to explore the lived experiences of small business owners who experienced failure. I was intrigued by the responses of the 10 small business owners who participated in the study. I learned that small businesses primarily supported most of the U. S communities through employment opportunities and household revenue. Almost every participant suffered a serious financial loss that continued to instill a sense of desperation to venture into any business sooner.

The lived experiences of 10 enhanced my understanding about the predominant causes of failure of small businesses. I was shocked to find that limited funding was the major cause of failure of small businesses against my expectation that lack of leadership played a major role in causing the phenomenon. I learned that the following factors in order of significance caused failure of small businesses; lack of knowledge and understanding, poor leadership, economic crisis poor business location, lack of motivation and inspiration, culture, size and poor Planning.

I also learned that data collection could be the most challenging part of the research journey because of serious limitations. The time was constrained, the topic and problem seemed to be too broad and endless, and sometimes the exercise could be costly from spending on travelling to making research materials and arrangements available. Nevertheless, I was proud the study findings contributed to the body of knowledge that not only enhanced the understanding but also could be significant to the field of research, leaders and the society as a whole.

I was truly inspired by the successful academic endeavors. The study's progress and the research logistics formed the basis and inspiration for my future research endeavors. It was a lesson learned that everything is possible with systematic determination. I am and will continue to be thankful and grateful for the University of Phoenix for facilitating the administrative logistics of my study. The journey was the dream come true!

References

Adamoniene, R., & Andriuscenka, J. (2007). The small and medium-sized enterprises: The aspects of appliance the principles of strategic management. *Economics & Management, 12,* 548-555. Retrieved from http:// archive.minfolit.lt/arch/17501/17820.pdf

Alvesson, M., & Sandberg, J. (2011). Generating research questions through problematization. *Academy of management review, 36*(2), 247-271. doi:10.5465/ AMR.2011.59330882

Amel, D. H., & Imen, A. ((2012). The entrepreneurial failure: Exploring links between the main causes of failure and the company life cycle. *International Journal of Business and Social Science, 3*(4), 189. Retrieved from http://www.ijbssnet.com/

Arasti, Z., Zandi, F., & Talebi, K. (2012). Exploring the effect of individual factors on business failure in Iranian new established small businesses. *International Business Research, 5*(4), 2-11. Retrieved from http://www.ccsenet.org/journal/ index.php/ibr

Armour, M., Rivaux, S. L., & Bell, H. (2009). Using context to build rigor. *Qualitative Social Work, 8*(1), 101-122. doi:10.1177/1473325008100424

Asare, S. D., Gopolang, B., & Mogotlhwane, O. (2012). Challenges facing SMEs in the adoption of ICT in B2B and B2C E-commerce. *International Journal of Commerce & Management, 22*(4), 272-285. doi:10.1108/10569211211284485

Aterido, R., Hallward-Driemeier, M., & Pages, C. (2011). Big constraints to small firms' growth? Business environment and employment across firms. *Economic Development and Cultural Change, 59*(3), 609-647. doi:10.1596/1813-9450-5032

Audretsch, D. (2012). Entrepreneurship research. *Management Decision, 50*(5), 755-764. doi:10.1108/00251741211227384

Avolio, B. J., & Yammarino, F. J. (Eds.) (2013). *Transformational and charismatic leadership: The road ahead.* (2nd ed.). Bingley, UK: Emerald.

Baldwin, J., Gray, T., Johnson, J., Proctor, G., Rafiquzzaman, M., & Sabourin, D. (1997). *Failing concerns: Business bankruptcy in Canada.* Retrieved from http://publications.gc.ca/Collection/Statcan/61-525-X/61-525-XIE1997001.pdf

Bandi, R., & Lefter, C. (2009). European policies for the stimulation of development of SMEs. *Bulletin of the Transilvania University of Brasov, V*(2), 23-26. Retrieved from http://webbut.unitbv.ro/bulletin/

Barkhuizen, G. (2008). Qualitative inquiry and research design: Choosing among five approaches (2nd ed.). [Review of book by J. Creswell]. *New Zealand Studies in Applied Linguistics, 14*(2), 98-99.

Baron, R. A., Franklin, R. J., & Hmieleski, K. M. (2013).Why entrepreneurs often experience low, not high, levels of stress: The joint effects of selection and psychological capital. *Journal of Management.* doi:10.1177/0149206313495411

Basit, T. (2003). Manual or electronic? The role of coding in qualitative data analysis. *Educational Research 45*(2), 143-154. DOI:10.1080/0013188032000133548.

Bass, B. M. (1990). *Bass & Stogdill's handbook of leadership: Theory, research, and managerial applications* (3rd ed.). New York, NY: The Free Press.

Beaver, G. (2003). Small business: Success and failure. *Strategic Change, 12*(3), 115. Retrieved from http://onlinelibrary.wiley.com/journal/10.1002/(ISSN)1099-1697

Beaver, G., & Jennings, P. (2005). Competitive advantage and entrepreneurial power: The dark side of entrepreneurship. *Journal of Small Business and Enterprise Development, 12*(1), 9. Retrieved from http://www.emeraldinsight.com/journal/ jsbed

Belinda, C. V., & Allan, G. B. (2014). From scratch to notch: Understanding private tutoring metamorphosis in the Philippines from the perspectives of cram school and formal school administrators. Education and Urban Society, 46(3), 287-311. doi:10.1177/0013124512439888

Beck, N., Bruderl, J., & Woywode, M. (2008). Momentum or deceleration? Theoretical and methodological reflections on the analysis of organizational change. *Academy of Management Journal, 51*(3), 413-435. doi:10.5465/AMJ.2008.32625943

Bernal, R. L. (1996). *Strategic global repositioning and future economic development in Jamaica.* Retrieved from http://ctrc.sice.oas.org/trc/Articles/Jamaica/ Strategic_JA_Bernal.pdf

Berte, E., Rodrigues, L. C., & Almeida, M. I. (2010). The lessons learned from the unique characteristics of small technology-based firms. *International Management Review, 6*(1), 62-70,110. doi:10.1016/S0956-5221(99)00010-X

Bloomberg, L., & Volpe, M. (2008). *Completing your qualitative dissertation: A roadmap from beginning to end.* Thousand Oaks, CA: Sage.

Bouchikhi, H. (1993). A constructivist framework for understanding entrepreneurship performance. *Organization Studies, 14*(4), 549. doi:10.1177/ 017084069301400405

Bracker, J. S., Keats, B. W., & Pearson, J. N. (1988). Planning and financial performance among small firms in a growth industry. *Strategic Management Journal, 9*(6), 591-603.

Briggs, W. (2013). Problem solving for small businesses. *Annals of Psychotherapy & Integrative Health, 16*(2), 14-16. Retrieved from http:// www.annalsofpsychotherapy.com/

Brouthers, K. D., Gelderman, M., & Arens, P. (2007). The influence of ownership on performance: Stakeholder and strategic contingency perspectives. *Schmalenbach Business Review, 59*(3), 225-242. Retrieved from http://www.sbr-online.de/

Brown, T. B., & Kimball, T. (2013). Cutting to live: A phenomenology of self-harm. *Journal of Marital and Family Therapy, 39*(2), 195-208. Retrieved from http://onlinelibrary.wiley.com/journal/10.1111/(ISSN)1752-0606

Business failure. (2014). *In BusinessDictionary.com.* Retrieved September 19, 2014 from www.businessdictionary.com/definition/business-failure.html

Byrne, M. (2009). *Understanding life experiences through a phenomenological approach to research.* Retrieved from http://findarticles.com/p/articles/mi_m0FSL/is_4_73/ ai_73308177/

Çakar, N., & Ertürk, A. (2010). Comparing innovation capability of small and medium-sized enterprises: Examining the effects of organizational culture and empowerment. *Journal of Small Business Management, 48*(3), 325-359. Retrieved http://onlinelibrary.wiley.com/journal/10.1111/(ISSN)1540-627X

Carmen M. Reinhart, Kenneth S. Rogoff (2009). *"This time is different: eight centuries of financial folly"*. Princeton University Press. p.30

Carreira, C., & Silva, F. (2010). No deep pockets: Some stylized empirical results on firms' financial constraints. *Journal of Economic Surveys, 24*(4), 731–753.

Christensen, L. B., Johnson, R. B., & Turner, L. A. (2011). *Research methods, design, and analysis* (11th ed.). Boston, MA: Allyn & Bacon.

City of San Jose. (2013). *Economic strategy.* Retrieved from http://www.sanjoseca.gov/ DocumentCenter/View/6826

Cobley, P. R. (2015). *Education programs and leadership training - countering the physiological and psychological effects of combat on infantry soldiers: A case study.* (Doctoral dissertation). Retrieved from ProQuest Dissertations & Theses Global. (Order No. 3681822).

Cochran, A. B. (1981). Small business mortality rates: A review of the literature. *Journal of Small Business Management, 19*(4), 50-59. Retrieved from http://onlinelibrary.wiley.com/journal/10.1111/(ISSN)1540-627X

Collins, J. (2003). Designing clinical research studies: Part I. *Urologic Nursing, 23*(5),

357. Retrieved from https://www.suna.org/unjCollins, J. (2005). Levels of 5 leadership: The triumph of humility and fierce resolve. *Harvard Business Review, 83*(7/8), 136-146. Retrieved from http://hbr.org/

Colaizzi, P. F. (1978). Psychological research as the phenomenologist views it. In R. S. Valle & M. King (Eds.), *Existential phenomenological alternatives for psychology* (pp. 48-71). New York, NY: Oxford University Press.

Conklin, T. A. (2007). Method or madness: Phenomenology of knowledge creator. *Journal of Management Inquiry, 16*(3), 275-287. Retrieved from http:// jmi.sagepub.com/

Creswell, J. W. (2002). *Educational research: Planning, conducting, and evaluating quantitative and qualitative research.* Upper Saddle River, NJ: Pearson Education, Inc.

Creswell, J. W. (2005). *Research design: Qualitative, quantitative, and mixed methods approaches* (2nd ed.). London, England: Sage.

Creswell, J. W. (2007). *Qualitative inquiry and research design: Choosing among five traditions* (2nd ed.). Thousand Oaks, CA: Sage.

Creswell, J. W. (2009). *Research design: Qualitative, quantitative, and mixed methods approaches* (3rd ed.). Los Angeles, CA: Sage.

Creswell, J. W. (2010). *Research design: Qualitative, quantitative, and mixed methods approaches.* Thousand Oaks, CA: Sage.

Creswell, J, W. (2012). *Qualitative inquiry and research design: Choosing among five approaches.* Thousand Oaks, CA: Sage.

Creswell, J. W., Hanson, W. E., Plano Clark, V. L., & Morales, A. (2007). Qualitative research designs: Selection and implementation. *Counseling Psychologist, 35*, 236-264. Doi:10.1177/0011000006287390

Creswell, J. W., & Plano Clark, V. L. (2007). *The mixed methods reader.* Thousand Oaks, CA: Sage.

Creswell, J. W., Plano Clark, V. L., Gutmann, M., & Hanson, W. (2010). Advanced mixed methods research: Designs. In A. Tashakkori & C. Teddie (Eds.), *Handbook of mixed methods in social and behavioral research* (pp. 619–637). Los Angeles, CA: Sage.

Cronin-Gilmore, J. (2012). Exploring marketing strategies in small businesses. *Journal of Marketing Development and Competitiveness, 6*(1), 96-107. Retrieved from http://www.na-businesspress.com/jmdcopen.html

Danuta, M. W., & Kristen, M. S. (2007). Phenomenology: An exploration. *Journal of Holistic Nursing, 25*(3), 172-180. doi:10.1177/0898010106295172

Darling, J., & Leffel, A. (2010). Developing the leadership team in an entrepreneurial venture: A case focusing on the importance of styles. *Journal of Small Business and Entrepreneurship, 23*(3), 355-371, 481. Retrieved from http://www.tandfonline.com/toc/rsbe20/current#.VByNzy5dVxs

Dasgupta, S., & Sanyal, D. (2010) A stitch in time saves nine: behind every major business failure lies an untold story. *Journal of Business Strategy Series, 11*(2), 100 - 106. doi:10.1108/17515631011026425

DeCaro, F., DeCaro, N., & Bowen-Thompson, F. (2010). An examination of leadership styles of minority business entrepreneurs: A case study of public contracts. *The Journal of Business and Economic Studies, 16*(2), 72-79. Retrieved from http://som.njit.edu/jbes/index.php

Discover the Network. (2011). *California's economic decline.* Retrieved from: http://www.discoverthenetworks.org/viewSubCategory.asp?id=1678

Divsalar, M., Firouzabadi, A., Sadeghi, M., Behrooz, A., & Alavi, A. (2011). Towards the prediction of business failure via computational intelligence techniques. *Expert Systems, 28*(3), 209-226. doi:10.1111/j.1468-0394.2011.00580.x

Dobbs, M., & Hamilton, R. T. (2007). Small business growth: Recent evidence and new directions. *International Journal of Entrepreneurial Behavior & Research, 13*(13), 296-322. Retrieved fromhttp://www.emeraldgrouppublishing.com/ ijebr.htm

Duff, P. A., & Seror, J. (2005). Computers and Qualitative Data Analysis: Paper, Pens, and Highlighters vs. Screen, Mouse, and Keyboard. *Tesol Quarterly journal 39* (2)   321–328. DOI: 10.2307/3588315 (http://dx.doi.org/ 10.2307/3588315).

Edmister, R. O. (1972). An empirical test of financial ratio analysis for small business failure prediction. *Journal of Financial & Quantitative Analysis, 7*(2), 1477-1493. Retrieved from http://journals.cambridge.org/action/ displayJournal?jid=JFQ

Edmond, J. (2011). Managing successful change. *Industrial and Commercial Training 43*(6), 349 - 353. DOI: 10.1108/00197851111160478

EDD and California Department of Finance. (2010). Performance of San Jose economy: 2004-2009. Retrieved from: http://www.sanjoseca.gov/DocumentCenter/View/ 6815

Ellis, J. (2012). New businesses then and now: *Success and failure. Arkansas Business, 29*(28), 14. Retrieved from https://store.arkansasbusiness.com/publications/view/ publication_id/1?gclid=CjwKEAjwqO-gBRCEyp2Fufm0lBAS-JAAZrX-5L7DgGXxq4RiqcQyySeZigtN7lRyKXyGZ5YIQ_k 61rBoCaojw_wcB

Emale, J. M. (2010). An examination of how conglomerates impact small-medium enterprises in their relationship. *Dissertation Abstracts International, 71*(05), 138A. (UMI No. 3407430)

Fard, H., Rostamy, A., & Taghiloo, H. (2009). How types of organizational cultures contribute in shaping learning organizations. Singapore Management Review, 31(1), 49-61. Retrieved from http://www.sim.edu.sg/resources/pages/ publications.aspx

Fink, K., & Ploder, C. (2009). Balanced system for knowledge process management in SMEs. *Journal of Enterprise Information Management, 22*, 36-50. doi:10.1108/174103909109228 13 161

Finlay, L. (2008). *Introducing phenomenological research.* Retrieved from www. lindafinlay.co.uk/An%20introduction%20to%20phenomenology%202008.doc

Franco, M. and Haase, H. (2010). Failure Factors in SME: A Qualitative Study from an Attributional Perspective. *International Entrepreneurship and Management Journal, 6*(4), 503-521.

Fisher, D. (2010). Leading a sustainable organization. The Journal for Quality and Participation, 32(4), 29-31. Retrieved from http://asq.org/pub/jqp/

Fredland, J. E., & Morris, C. E. (1976). A cross section analysis of small business failure. *American Journal of Small Business, 1*(1), 7-18. Retrieved from http:// www.bsu.edu/mcobwin/ajb/?p=250

Frey, R. S. (2001). Knowledge management, proposal development, and small businesses. *The Journal of Management Development, 20*(1), 38-54. DOI: http:// dx.doi.org/10.1108/02621710110365041

Gaan, N., & Bhoon, K. S. (2012). Transformational HR through employee engagement – A case. Vilakshan: *The XIMB Journal of Management, 9*(2), 147-160.

Ganster, S. H. (2007). Strategies for SMEs. *China Business Review, 34*(1), 38-41. Retrieved from http://www.chinabusinessreview.com/

Gaskill, L. R., Van Auken, E. H., & Manning, R. (1993). A factor analytic study of the perceived causes of small business failure. *Journal of Small Business Management, 31*(4), 18-31. Retrieved from http://onlinelibrary.wiley.com/journal/10.1111/(ISSN)1540-627X

Gentry, W. A. (2006). Human resource officers' opinions of their own companies and "the big three": A qualitative study profiling businesses in a southeastern city. *Organization Development Journal, 24*(2), 33. Retrieved from: http://search.proquest.com/openview/238b1acf4a65812827281b434b614b1c/ 1?pq-origsite=gscholar

Giles, D. (2007). Humanizing the researcher: The influence of phenomenological research on a teacher educator. International Journal of Pedagogies and Learning, 3(1), 6-12. Retrieved from http://jpl.e-contentmanagement.com/

Gilmore, A., Carson, D., & O'Donnell, A. (2004). Small business owner-managers and their attitude to risk. *Marketing Intelligence & Planning, 22*(2/3), 349. Retrieved from http://www.emeraldinsight.com/loi/mip

Habaradas, R. (2008). SME development and technology upgrading In Malaysia: Lessons for the Philippines. *Journal of International Business Research: Special Issue, 1*(7), 89-116. Retrieved from http://www.alliedacademies.org/public/journals/journaldetails.aspx?jid=15

Hammond, J., Keeney, R., & Raiffa, H. (1999). Smart choices: A practical guide to making better decisions. Harvard Business School Press Risk Analysis: *An International Journal, 32*(7), 1113-1116. doi:10.1111/j.1539-6924.2012.01865.x

Harold, S. T., Gurpreet, S. B., & Sajid, A. (2011). A success versus failure prediction model for small businesses in Singapore. *American Journal of Business, 26*(1), 50 - 64. doi:10.1108/19355181111124106

Harrison, S., & Parish, C. (2008). R*eview of regulator criticises poor leadership and communication. Nursing Standard* (through 2013), 22(41), 10. Retrieved from http://search.proquest.com/docview/219843732?accountid=458

Haverkamp, B. E., & Young, R. A. (2007). Paradigms, purpose, and the role of the literature: Formulating a rationale for qualitative investigations. *The Counseling Psychologist, 35*(2), 265-294. Retrieved from http://tcp.sagepub.com/

Headd, B. (2003). Redefining business success: Distinguishing between closure and failure. *Small Business Economics, 21*(1), 51. Retrieved from http:// link.springer.com/journal/11187

Heady, R., Maples, G., & Greco, A. (2005). *Cost engineering for small businesses. AACE International Transactions,* DE41-DE45. Retrieved from http://www.aacei.org/

Helsinki University of Technology. (2008). *Doctoral studies.* Retrieved from http:// www.tkk.fi/en/studies/doctoral/

Hersey, P., & Blanchard, K. H. (1969). Life cycle theory of leadership. *Training & Development Journal, 23,* 26-34. Retrieved from http:// www.traininganddevelopmentjournal.com/

Hertz, L. (1982). *In search of a small business definition.* Washington, D.C: University Press of America.

Hoepfl, M. C. (1997). Choosing qualitative research: A primer for technology education researchers. *Journal of Technology Education, 9*(1), 47-86. Retrieved from: http://scholar.lib.vt.edu/ejournals/JTE/

Holland, R. (1998). *Planning against a business failure.* Retrieved from http://
frrl.files.wordpress.com/2009/09/smallbusiness_planninga-gainstabusinessfailure_ uoftennessee.pdf

Holloway, I., & Wheeler, S. (2009). *Qualitative research in nursing and healthcare* (3rd ed.). West Sussex, UK: John Wiley and Sons.

Holt, G. D. (2013). Construction business failure: Conceptual synthesis of causal agents. *Construction Innovation, 13*(1), 50 - 76. doi:10.1108/14714171311296057

Hunter, M. G. (2011). Understanding the common causes of small business failures: A qualitative study. *Journal of Applied Management and Entrepreneurship, 16*(1), 86-103. Retrieved from http://www.whitneypress.com/jame/

Hussain, I., Si, S., Xie, X. M., & Wang, L. (2010). Comparative study on impact of internal and external CFFS on SMES. *Journal of Small Business and Entrepreneurship, 23*, 637-648. Retrieved from http://www.jsbe.com/

Ibrahim, N. A., Angelidis, J. P., & Parsa, F. (2004). The status of planning in small business. *American Business Review, 22*(2), 52. Retrieved from https://business.illinois.edu/profile/journals-ambure/

Islam, M. A., Khan, M. A., Obaidullah, A. Z. M., Alam, M. S. (2011). Effect of entrepreneur and firm characteristics on the business success of small and medium enterprises (SMEs) in Bangladesh. *International Journal of Business and Management, 6*(3), 289-299. Retrieved from http://www.ccsenet.org/journal/ index.php/ijbm

Johns Hopkins University. (2008). *Managing your qualitative data: Five steps.* Retrieved from http://ocw.jhsph.edu/courses/qualitativedataanalysis/PDFs/Session2.pdf

Johnson, C. H. (2014). Reflections on leadership. *Naval War College Review, 67*(1), 135-144.

Jones, R., & Noble, G. (2007). Grounded theory and management research: A lack of integrity? Qualitative Research in Organizations and Management: *An International Journal, 2*(2), 84-103. Retrieved from http:// www.emeraldinsight.com/journal/qrom

Joshi, A., Lazarova, M. B., & Liao, H. (2009). Getting everyone on board: The role of inspirational leadership in geographically dispersed teams. *Organization Science, 20*(1), 240-252. doi:10.1287/orsc.1080.0383

Jui-Chen, C., & Silverthorne, C. (2005). Leadership effectiveness, leadership style and employee readiness. *Leadership & Organization Development Journal, 26*(3), 280-288. doi:0.1108/01437730510600652

Kamal, M. (2009). Effects of information technology interventions in micro-enterprises on development. *Dissertation Abstracts International, 70*(06), 259A. (UMI No. 3359240).

Kamisan, A. P., & King, B. E. M. (2013). Transactional and transformational leadership: A comparative study of the difference between tony fernandes (airasia) and idris jala (malaysia airlines) leadership styles from 2005-2009. *International Journal of Business and Management, 8*(24), 107-116. Retrieved from http:// www.ccsenet.org/journal/index.php/ijbm

Kantabutra, S. (2009). Toward a behavioral theory of vision in organizational settings. *Leadership & Organization Development Journal, 30*(4), 319 – 337. Retrieved from http://www.emeraldgrouppublishing.com/products/journals/ journals.htm?id=LODJ

Karanja, T., Muturi, P., Mukabi, M., Kabata, D., Susan, W., & Mercy, K. (2013). Small business management. *International Journal of Business and Social Science, 4*(16). Retrieved from http://www.ccsenet.org/journal/index.php/ijbm

Kayemuddin, M. D. (2012). Leadership in small business in Bangladesh. *International Journal of Entrepreneurship, 16,* 25-35. Retrieved from http://www.alliedacademies.org/public/journals/JournalDetails.aspx?jid=7

Kempster, S., & Parry, K. (2014). Charismatic leadership through the eyes of followers. *Strategic HR Review, 13*(1), 20 - 23. doi:10.1108/SHR-07-2013-0076

Kobe, K. (2007a). *Frequently asked questions.* Retrieved from http://www.sba.gov/sites/ default/files/sbfaq.pdf

Kobe, K. (2007b). *The small business share of the GDP, 1998-2004* (SBAHQ-05-M-0413). Washington, DC: U.S. Small Business Administration.

Kouzes, J. M., & Posner, B. Z. (2012). *The leadership challenge* (5th ed.). San Francisco, CA: Jossey-Bass.

LandLearn NSW. (2010). *Newsletter, Update term 2.* Retrieved from http://www.landlearnnsw.org.au/__data/assets/pdf_file/0005/331925/landlearn-nsw-newsletter-term2-2010.pdf

Lappalainen, J., & Niskanen, M. (2013). Behavior and attitudes of small family firms towards different funding sources. *Journal of Small Business and Entrepreneurship, 26*(6), 579-599. doi:10.1080/08276331.2014.892309.

Lawrence, W. W. (2010). *Developing a small business in* Jamaica. Retrieved from http://cbhm.ncu.edu.jm/downloadable-docs/Dr_William_Lawrence-Developing_Small_Business.pdf.

Lee, B., Riche, N., Karlson, A., & Carpendale, S., (2010). Spark-Clouds Visualizing Trends in Tag Clouds. *IEEE Transactions on Visualization and Computer Graphics, 16*(6), 1182–1189. Retrieved from: http://ieeexplore.ieee.org/stamp/stamp.jsp?tp=&arnumber=5613457&isnumber=5613414

Leedy, P. D., & Ormrod, J. E. (2005). *Practical research: Planning and design* (8th ed.). Upper Saddle River, NJ: Merrill-Prentice Hall.

Leedy, P. D., & Ormrod, J. E. (2010). *Practical research: Planning and design* (9th ed.). Upper Saddle River, NJ: Prentice Hall.

Liao, J., Welsch, H., & Moutray, C. H. (2009). Start-up resources and entrepreneurial discontinuance the case of nascent entrepreneurs. *Journal of Small Business Strategy, 19*(2), 1-15. Retrieved from http://smallbusinessinstitute.biz/page-1259165?

Lincoln, Y. S., & Guba, E. G. (1985). *Naturalistic inquiry.* Newbury Park, CA: Sage Publications

Longley, R. (2009). *Small business drives U.S. economy: Provides jobs for over half of nation's private workforce.* Retrieved from http://usgovinfo.about.com/od/smallbusiness/a/sbadrives.htm

Lu, X. (2004). Surveying the topic of "effective leadership." *The Journal of American Academy of Business, 5*(1/2), 125-127. Retrieved from http://www.jaabc.com/journal.htm

Lusky, H., & Lusky, M. (2006, April 7). *Start up a business - but also plan for its ending.* Retrieved from: http://denver.bizjournals.com/denver/stories/2016/04/10/ smallb4.html

Lussier, R. N., & Halabi, C. E. (2010). A three-country comparison of the business success versus failure prediction model. *Journal of Small Business Management, 48*(3), 360-377. doi:10.111/j1540-627X.2010.00298.x

Lyles, M. A., Baird, I. S., Orris, J. B., & Kuratko, D. F. (1995). Formalized planning in small business: Increasing strategic choices. *Journal of Small Business Management, 31*(2), 38-50. Retrieved from http://onlinelibrary.wiley.com/ journal/10.1111/(ISSN)1540-627X

Maes, J., Sels, L., & Roodhooft, F. (2005). Modeling the link between management practices and financial performance. Evidence from small construction companies. *Small Business Economics, 25*(1), 17. doi:10.1007/sl 1 187-005-4255-y

Maryland Chamber of Commerce. (2004). Small business. Retrieved from http:// www.mdchamber.org

McCartan-Quinn, D., & Carson, D. (2003). Issues which impact upon marketing in the small firm. *Small Business Economics, 21*(2), 201. Retrieved from http://link.springer.com/journal/11187

McKinney, K. D. (2009). *A phenomenological exploration of leadership characteristics of small business owner-founders.* (Doctoral dissertation). Retrieved from ProQuest Dissertations and Theses database (Order No. 3371532).

Madurapperuma, W. (2011, January 1). Does culture impact on Social networks of ethnic, small business entrepreneurs?. In *International Council for Small business* (ICSB) World Conference Proceedings (p. 1). Retrieved from: http:// repository.kln.ac.lk/xmlui/bitstream/handle/123456789/6682/does%20culture.pdf ?sequence=1

Merlin conjures wrong image of business failure. (2011, 03). Retrieved from http:// www.ccrmagazine.com/index.php?option=com_content&task=view&id=4442

Moustakas, C. E. (1994). *Phenomenological research methods.* Thousand Oaks, CA: Sage.

Moustakas, C. (1996). *Phenomenological research methods.* Thousand Oaks, CA: Sage.

Mueller, S., & Stegmaier, J. (2015). Economic failure and the role of plant age and size. *Small Business Economics, 44*(3), 621-638. doi:http://dx.doi.org/ 10.1007/s11187-014-9616-y

Nadim, A., & Lussier, R. N. (2010). Sustainability as a small business competitive strategy. *Journal of Small Business Strategy, 21*(2), 79-95. Retrieved from http://smallbusinessinstitute.biz/page-1259165?

Nanjundaswamy, T. S., & Swamy, D. R. (2014). *Leadership styles. Advances in Management, 7*(2), 57-62.

Neuman, W. L. (2003). *Social research methods: Qualitative and quantitative approaches* (5th ed.). Boston, MA: Allyn and Bacon.

Neuman, W. L. (2005). *Social research methods: Qualitative and quantitative approaches* (6th ed.). Upper Saddle River, NJ: Prentice Hall.

Neuman, W. L. (2006). *Social research methods: Qualitative and quantitative approaches* (6th ed.). Boston, MA: Allyn & Bacon.

Nguyen, P. A., & Robinson, A. G. (2010). Managing continuous improvement in Vietnam: Unique challenges and approaches to overcome them. *The Quality Management Journal, 17*(2), 27-41.

Ong, S., Yap, V.C., Khong, R. W. L. (2011). Corporate failure prediction: A study of public listed companies in Malaysia. *Managerial Finance, 37*(6), 553-64.

Patton, M. Q. (2002). *Qualitative evaluation and research methods* (3rd ed.). Thousand Oaks, CA: Sage.

Perry, S. C. (2001). The relationship between written business plans and the failure of small businesses in the U.S. *Journal of Small Business Management, 39*(3), 201-208.

Perry, D. (2009). *Roadmap for dividend and capital conservation. In Finance, (1),* 50-51. Peterson, R. A., Albaum, G., &

Kozmetsky, G. (1986). The public definition of small business, Journal of Small Business Management, 24(3),63. doi:10.1111/(ISSN)1540-627X

Phipps, S. T. A., Prieto, L. C., & Verma, S. (2012). Holding the helm: Exploring the influence of transformational leadership on group creativity, and the moderating role of organizational learning culture. *Journal of Organizational Culture, Communications & Conflict, 16*(2), 145-156. Retrieved from: https://www.researchgate.net/publication/288655346_Holdingsthe_h elm_Exploring_the _influence_of_transformational_leadership_on_group_creativity_and_the_moder ating_role_of_organizational_learning_culture

Pringle, J., Hendry, C., & McLafferty, E. (2011). Phenomenological approaches: Challenges and choices. *Nurse Researcher, 18*(2), 7-18. Retrieved from http:// rcnpublishing.com/journal/nr

Rabino, S., Simoni, C., & Zanni, L. (2008). Small & medium gold & fashion enterprises (SMEs) in Arezzo, Italy: Competitive challenges and strategic implications. *Journal of Global Marketing, 21*(2), 141-159. Retrieved from http://www.tandfonline.com/toc/wglo20/current#.VBycuC5dVxs

Reynolds, J. (2010, February 28). *A time for change: How to grow and develop the economy. The Jamaica Gleaner.* Retrieved from http://www.jamaica-gleaner. com/gleaner/20100228/cleisure/cleisure2.html

Ricardo Vinícius, D. J., & de Souza, A. A. (2013). Company's acquisition as A factor of change on the management control system: A strategic analysis from the perspective of the contingency theory. *Revista Universo Contabil, 9*(3), 75-103. doi:10.4270/ruc.2013323: Retrieved from http://www.furb.br/universocontabil/

Rietsema, K. W., & Watkins, D. V. (2012). Beyond leadership. *International Journal of Business and Social Science, 3*(4) Retrieved from http://www.ijbssnet.com/

Rogoff, E. G., Lee, M., & Suh, D. (2004). "Who done it?" Attributions by entrepreneurs and experts of the factors that cause and impede small business success. *Journal of Small Business Management, 42*(4), 364.doi 0.1111/j.1540-627X.2004.00117.x

Rudestam, K. E., & Newton, R. R. (2007). *Surviving your dissertation: A comprehensive guide to content and process* (3rd ed.). Thousand Oaks, CA: Sage.

Samad, N., Abdullah, Z., Jusoff, K., Mohamad, Z., & Nair, G. (2010). Globalization sustainability of Malaysian small and medium-sized enterprises (SMEs) through gaining competitive advantages. Interdisciplinary *Journal of Contemporary Research in Business, 2*(1), 399-413. Retrieved from http://www.ijcrb.com/

San Jose City. (2010). *Government official report.* Retrieved from http:// www.sanjoseca.gov/DocumentCenter/Index/866; www.labormarket/edd.ca.gov

San Jose City. (2013). *City of San Jose's Small Business Development Commission* (Commission) - SBDC. Retrieved from http://www.sanjoseca.gov/ DocumentCenter/View/1362

Sardana, D., & Scott-Kemmis, D. (2010). Who learns what? A
study based on entrepreneurs from biotechnology new ventures. *Journal of Small Business Management, 48*(3), 441-468.
Retrieved from http://onlinelibrary.wiley.com/ jour-
nal/10.1111/(ISSN)1540-627X

Scanlon, J. (2002). Robert Sokolowski, introduction to phenomenology. *Husserl Studies, 18*(1), 83-88.
doi:10.1023/A:1014076509452

Schehr, K. J. (2011). *FEMA disaster assistance and the mitigation
of small business failure after hurricane Katrina: A correla-
tion study.* (Doctoral dissertation). Retrieved from ProQuest
Dissertations & Theses. (Order No. 3468111).

Shaoming, C., Stough, R., & Jackson, R. (2009). Measuring and
building high-quality entrepreneurship: A research prospectus.
Innovation: *The European Journal of Social Sciences, 22,*
329-340. doi:10.1080/13511610903399088

Shneiderman, B., & Plaisant, C. (2009). *Tree-maps for space-con-
strained visualization of hierarchies - including the History of
Treemap Research at the University of Maryland.* Retrieved
from http://www.cs.umd.edu/hcil/treemap-history/

Simmons, J. (2007). *Small business: A phenomenological study of
small business failure in Maryland.* (Doctoral dissertation).
Retrieved from ProQuest Dissertations and Theses. (Order No.
329921).

Singh, R. K., Garg, S. K., & Deshmukh, S. G. (2008). *Strategy development by SMEs for competitiveness: A review.* Bench-
marking, 15, 525-547. doi:10.1108/1463577 0810903132 171

Skeete, V., Boodraj, G., Kiddoe, G., Lawla, J., Marcelle-Peart, L.,
& Williams-Myers, C. (2008). *Global entrepreneurship monitor: 2008 Jamaica report.* Retrieved from http://www.gem-
consortium.org/docs/download/541

Snap Surveys Ltd. (2009). *Qualitative vs. quantitative research.* Retrieved from http://
www.snapsurveys.com/techadvqualquant.shtml

Sokolowski, R. (2000). *Introduction to phenomenology.* New York, NY: Cambridge University Press.

Sosik, J. J., & Cameron, J. C. (2010). Character and authentic transformational leadership behavior: Expanding the ascetic self toward others. Consulting Psychology Journal: *Practice and Research, 62*(4), 251-269. doi:10.1037/a0022104

Storey, D. J. (1994). *Understanding the small business sector.* London, ENG: Routledge.

Storey, D. J., Keasey, K., Watson, R., Wynarczyk, P. (1987). *The performance of small firms: Profits, jobs and failures.* London, England: Croom Helm.

Strauss, A., & Corbin, J. (1990). *Basics of qualitative research: Grounded theory procedures and techniques.* London, England: Sage.

Strong, T., Pyle, N. R., Devries, C., Johnston, D. N., & Foskett, A. J. (2008). Meaning making lenses in counseling: Discursive, hermeneutic-phenomenological, and autoethnographics perspectives. *Canadian Journal of Counseling, 42*(2), 117-130. Retrieved from http://cjc-rcc.ucalgary.ca/cjc/index.php/rcc

Swinton-Douglas, V. (2010). *A phenomenological study of employee engagement in the workplace: The employee perspective* (Doctoral Dissertation). Retrieved from ProQuest Dissertations and Theses database. (Order No. 3421055).

Tambunan, T. (2008). SME development, economic growth, and government intervention in a developing country: The Indonesian story. *Journal of International Entrepreneurship, 6,* 147-167. doi:10.1007/s10843-008-0025-7

Tate, C.E. Jr., Megginson, C. R., Scott. Jr., & Trueblood, L. R. (1978). *Successful small business management.* Anaheim, CA: Business Publications, Inc.

Temtime, Z. T., Chinyoka, S. V., & Shunda, J. P. W. (2004). A decision tree approach for 128 integrating small business assistance schemes. *The Journal of Management Development, 23*(5/6), 563. Retrieved from http://www.emeraldinsight.com/journal/jmd

Teng, H. S. S. T., & Bhatia, G. S., & Anwar, S. (2011).A success versus failure prediction model for small businesses in Singapore, *American Journal of Business, 26*(1), 50 - 64. doi:10.1108/19355181111124106

Thompson, J. L., & Martin, F. (2010), Strategic management: Awareness and change (6th ed.). Hampshire, England: Cengage Learning.

Tseng, C. C. (2010). *The effects of learning organization practices on organizational commitment and effectiveness for small and medium-sized enterprises in Taiwan.* (Doctoral dissertation). Retrieved from ProQuest Dissertations and Theses. (Order No. 3411883).

Tserng, H. P., Liao, H., Tsai, L. K., & Chen, P. (2011). Predicting contractor default with option-based credit models – models' performance and comparison with financial ratio models. *Journal of Construction Engineering and Management, 136*(6),412-20. doi:10.1061/(ASCE)CO.1943-7862.0000311

Tuleasca, L. (2012). The criteria for determining the business failure. Acta Universitatis Danubius: *Juridica, 8*(1), 33. 20. Retrieved from http://journals.univ-danubius.ro/index.php/juridica

Ucbasaran, D., Shepard, D. A., Lockett, A., & Lyon, S. J. (2013). Life after business failure: The process and consequences of business failure for entrepreneurs. *Journal of Management. 39*(1) 163-202. doi:10.1177/0149206312457823

United States Census Bureau. (2014). Statistics of U.S. businesses (SUSB) main. Retrieved from https://www.census.gov/econ/susb/

United States Small Business Administration: Office of Advocacy. (2005). Small business profiles for the states and territories. Retrieved from http://archive.sba.gov/advo/research/sb_econ2005.pdf

United States Small Business Administration (USSBA). (2011). Frequently asked questions. (Research fact sheet). Retrieved from http://www.sba.gov.site/default/ files/sbfaq.pdf

U.S. Department of Commerce. (2013). Statistics about business size (including small business) from the U.S. Census Bureau. Retrieved from http://www.census.gov/econ/smallbus.html

Van Manen, M. (1990). *Researching the lived experience: Human science for an action sensitive pedagogy.* Albany, NY: State University of New York Press.

Van Maanen, J., Dabbs, J. M., Jr., & Faulkner, R. R. (1982). V*arieties of qualitative research.* Beverly Hills, CA: Sage.

Van Teijlingen, E., & Hundley, V. (2001). The importance of pilot studies. *Social Research Update, 35.*

Vieira, E. S. (2014). Corporate risk in family businesses under economic crisis. *Innovar, 24*(53), 61-73. Retrieved from DOI: http://dx.doi.org/10.15446/ innovar.v24n53.43909

Visser, D. J., Coning, T. J., & Smit, E (2005). The relationship between the characteristics of the transformational leader and the entrepreneur in South African SMEs. *South African Journal of Business Management, 36*(3), 51-64. Retrieved from http://reference.sabinet.co.za/sa_epublication/busman

Walker, W. (2007). Ethical considerations in phenomenological research. *Nurse Researcher, 14*(3), 36-45. doi:10.1111/j.1547-
5069.2001.00093.x

Watson, J., & Everett, J. (1996). Small business failure rates:
Choice of definition and the size effect. *Journal of Entrepreneurial and Small Business Finance, 5*(3), 272-285.

Weinreich, N. K. (2006). *Integrating quantitative and qualitative
methods in social marketing research.* Retrieved from
http://www.social-marketing.com/ research.html

Will, M. (2008). Talking about the future within an SME: Corporate
foresight and the potential contributions to sustainable development. *Management of Environmental Quality, 19*, 234-242.
doi:10.1108/14777830810856618

Willis, J. W. (2007). *Foundations of qualitative research: Interpre-
tative and critical approaches.* Thousand Oaks, CA: Sage.

Wojnar, D., & Swanson, K. (2007). Phenomenology. An exploration. *Journal of Holistic Nursing, 25*, 172-180. Retrieved
from http://jhn.sagepub.com/

Woods, M. (2011). *Interviewing for research and analyzing qualitative data: An overview.* Retrieved from
http://owll.massey.ac.nz/pdf/interviewing-for-research-and-
analysing-qualitative-data.pdf

Wu, J., Song, J., & Zeng, C. (2008). An empirical evidence of small
business financing in China. *Management Research News, 31,*
959. doi:10.1108/01409170810920666

Wray, N., Markovic, M., & Manderson, L. (2007). Researcher saturation: The impact of data triangulation and intensive-research
practices on the researcher and qualitative research process.
Qual Health Res, 17, 1392-1402. doi:10.1177/
1049732307308308

Yallapragada, R. R., & Bhuiyan, M. (2011). Small business entrepreneurships in the United States. *Journal of Applied Business Research, 27*(6), 117-122. Retrieved from http://www.scimagojr.com/journalsearch.php?q=100147315&tip=sid

Yin, R. K. (1993). *Applications of case study research: Applied Social research methods series* (2nd. ed.). Thousand Oaks, CA: Sage.

Yin, R. K. (2009). Case study research: Designs and methods. Thousand Oaks, CA: Sage.

Yu, M. (2010). High-performance human resource practices, entrepreneurship and entrepreneurial performance: A study in Taiwanese SMEs. *The Business Review, Cambridge, 15*(2), 117-124. Retrieved from http://www.jaabc.com/brc.html

Zecchini, S., & Ventura, M. (2009). The impact of public guarantees on credit to SMEs. *Small Business Economics, 32*, 191-206. doi:10.1007/s11187-007-9077

Ziegler, M., Paulus, T., & Woodside, M. (2006). Creating a climate of engagement in a blended learning environment. *Journal of Interactive Learning Research, 17*(3), 295. Retrieved from http://www.aace.org/pubs/jilr/

Appendix A
Semi-Structured Interview Questions

The central research question and sub-research questions will be aligned and supported by the following semi-structured open-ended interview questions. The interview questions will be portioned into four key sections: (a) unique characteristics of small business, (b) leadership, and (c) non-leadership factors. Every section includes questions about the perception of the participant pertaining the failure of small business in San Jose, California.

IQ1: How can you explain your lived experiences about the unique features common to small businesses that definitely contribute to failure of small businesses?

IQ2: What is your perception about the common features that cause failure of small businesses are more distinct to small businesses than large businesses?

IQ3: What is your perception and interpretation of small business characteristics causing failure of small businesses?

IQ4: What is your perception about leadership contributing to failure of small businesses?

IQ5: What is your perception about lack of knowledge contributing to failure of small businesses?

IQ6: What is your perception about the ways leadership impacts your capacity to prevent failure of small businesses?

IQ7: To what extent do you believe that the increasing failure rate trend of small businesses affect adversely the economy?.

IQ8: In what ways do you perceive leadership as significant or insignificant in endeavors to prevent failure of small businesses?

IQ9: How can you explain the extent of your belief in the ability of a leader to motivate and inspire employees affects the ability to prevent the failure of small businesses?

IQ10: What is your perception and explanation about non-leadership factors, such as small business location, size, planning, and funding contributing to failure of small businesses?

IQ11: How do you perceive and explain small business location contributing to failure of small businesses?

IQ12: How do you perceive and explain the size of small businesses contributing to failure of small businesses?

IQ13: How do you perceive and explain culture of small businesses contributing to failure of small businesses?

IQ14: What is your perception and explanation of small business owner's difficulty in acquiring funding affects the ability to prevent failure of small businesses?

IQ15: To what extent do you believe poor planning by owner leader of a small business affects the ability to prevent failure of small businesses?

IQ16: To what extent do you believe that the unique feature of small business owners operating with limited resources results in inevitable failure at times of financial crisis?

Appendix B

Informed Consent: Participants 18 Years of Age and Older

Dear Participant,

I am a student at the University of Phoenix working on a Doctoral Dissertation. I am conducting a research study entitled Failure of Small Business in San Jose, California: A qualitative Phenomenological Study. The purpose of the research study is to explore the lived experiences of small business owners who experienced failure small business to understand the predominant cause of small business failure in San Jose, California. Your interview participation will be voluntary and involve approximately 60 minutes responding to 15 questions. The participation in the study is and withdrawal at any time is optional without any benefit loss to yourself or penalty. The results of the research study may be published, but your name will not be used and confidentiality of your results will be maintained.

In this research, there are no foreseeable risks to you. Although there may be no direct benefit to you, the possible benefit of your participation is a contribution to the body of knowledge in this emerging field of inquiry and perhaps insights that may be leveraged by other leaders in your role. Please email me xxxx if you voluntarily accept to participate in the study. Please sign this document below, and I will pick it up prior to our scheduled interview. Contact me please at xxxx for any questions concerning the research study.

As a participant in this study, you should understand the following:

1. You may decline to participate or withdraw from participation at any time without consequences.

2. If you decide to withdraw from the study, you will be sent a written statement through email to confirm your withdrawal before the interview begins.

3. During the interview, if you decide to withdraw, the researcher will end the interview and cancel all documentation (i.e., completed and signed). You will be sent a written statement through email to confirm your withdrawal during the interview.

4. After the interview, if you decide to withdraw from the study, you could contact the researcher via email within a period of 3 days after the interview is completed. All documentation (i.e., hard and soft copies) will be destroyed immediately. You will be informed that the data collected will not be included in the study and will be sent a written statement through email immediately to confirm your withdrawal after the interview.

5. Your identity will be kept confidential.

6. Evans N. Ongaga, the researcher, will thoroughly explain the parameters of the research study and address all of your questions and concerns.

7. If the interviews are recorded, you will be required to grant permission for the researcher, Evans N. Ongaga, to digitally record the interview. You understand that the information from the recorded interviews may be transcribed. The researcher will structure a coding process to assure anonymity.

8. Data will be stored in a secure and locked area. The data will be held for a period of 7 years, and then destroyed.

9. The research results will be used for publication.

"By signing this form you acknowledge that you understand the nature of the study, the potential risks to you as a participant, and the means by which your identity will be kept confidential. Your signature on this form also indicates that you are 18 years old or older and that you give your permission to voluntarily serve as a participant in the study described."

Signature of the interviewee _______________________________ Date _______________

Signature of the researcher _______________________________ Date _______________

Appendix C
REQUEST FOR PARTICIPATION

Dear Small Business Owner-Leader,

My name is Evans N. Ongaga, and I am a doctoral student at the University of Phoenix in the Doctor of Business Management (Organizational Leadership) program. I have decided to write my dissertation on the failure of small businesses in San Jose, California. Specifically, as the owner leader of small business who failed, I want to conduct a research on the lived experiences of small business owners who experienced failure of their small businesses in San Jose, California. I value the unique contribution of small businesses to our communities and the role you play in decision-making of the business. I will be delighted if you possibly decide to participate in my study.

The purpose of this letter is to invite you to participate in the research on failure of small business. Your organization, and you as an owner, significantly contribute to San Jose's economy by creating of employment opportunities and technology. The results of the study will be shared with you as soon as the research is approved.

The criteria for you to participate in this research study is below:
    (a) Your organization employs 1-50 employees.
    (b) You have owned a small business for at least 5 years.
    (c) You have experienced small business failure.

If your organization meets the above listed criteria and you are willing to participate in a 1-hour face-to-face interview, please contact me using the contact information below.

Sincerely,
Evans N. Ongaga
Email: xxxx
Cell phone: xxxx

Appendix D
Letter of Appreciation to Participate

Letter of Appreciation to Participate

Dear Prospective Participant,

This letter serves as an appreciation for your interest in participating in my research on failure of small business in San Jose, California. I appreciate and value your participation in my dissertation research and look forward for our interview. This letter serves the purpose of securing your signature on the attached form of consent.

Please contact me at email: xxxx or tel. xxxx if you have any questions before committing your signature on the consent forms. Please self-address, and return the form of consent in the stamped envelope. I will schedule one-on-one interview with you as soon as I receive the returned and signed form of consent from you.

Sincerely,
Evans Ongaga

Appendix E
Word Frequency Query - Summary

Word	Length	Count	Weighted Percentage (%)
Area	4	9	0.13
Community	9	9	0.13
Finances	8	9	0.13
Harder	6	9	0.13
Leads	5	9	0.13
Capital	7	10	0.15
Characteristics	15	10	0.15
Concerning	10	10	0.15
Distinct	8	10	0.15
Endeavors	9	10	0.15
Experienced	11	10	0.15
Insignificant	13	10	0.15
Interpret	9	10	0.15
Interpretation	14	10	0.15
Interview	9	10	0.15
Meaning	7	10	0.15
Needed	6	10	0.15
Operate	7	10	0.15
Therefore	9	10	0.15
Belief	6	11	0.16
Causing	7	11	0.16
Feature	7	11	0.16
Impacts	7	11	0.16
Income	6	11	0.16
Less	4	11	0.16
Market	6	11	0.16
Services	8	11	0.16

Advertisement	13	12	0.18
Difficulties	12	12	0.18
Family	6	12	0.18
Important	9	12	0.18
Plan	4	12	0.18
Start	5	12	0.18
Affect	6	13	0.19
Difficulty	10	13	0.19
Feel	4	13	0.19
Needs	5	13	0.19
Place	5	13	0.19
Proper	6	13	0.19
Succeed	7	13	0.19
Time	4	13	0.19
Well	4	13	0.19
Cause	5	14	0.21
Loans	5	14	0.21
Rate	4	14	0.21
Trend	5	14	0.21
Adversely	9	15	0.22
Capacity	8	15	0.22
Inspire	7	15	0.22
Number	6	15	0.22
Think	5	15	0.22
Definitely	10	16	0.24
Increasing	10	16	0.24
Inevitable	10	16	0.24
Sales	5	16	0.24
Make	4	17	0.25
Motivate	8	17	0.25
Product	7	17	0.25
Products	8	17	0.25
Times	5	17	0.25
Lead	4	18	0.27

Advertisement	13	12	0.18
Difficulties	12	12	0.18
Family	6	12	0.18
Important	9	12	0.18
Plan	4	12	0.18
Start	5	12	0.18
Affect	6	13	0.19
Difficulty	10	13	0.19
Feel	4	13	0.19
Needs	5	13	0.19
Place	5	13	0.19
Proper	6	13	0.19
Succeed	7	13	0.19
Time	4	13	0.19
Well	4	13	0.19
Cause	5	14	0.21
Loans	5	14	0.21
Rate	4	14	0.21
Trend	5	14	0.21
Adversely	9	15	0.22
Capacity	8	15	0.22
Inspire	7	15	0.22
Number	6	15	0.22
Think	5	15	0.22
Definitely	10	16	0.24
Increasing	10	16	0.24
Inevitable	10	16	0.24
Sales	5	16	0.24
Make	4	17	0.25
Motivate	8	17	0.25
Product	7	17	0.25
Products	8	17	0.25
Times	5	17	0.25
Lead	4	18	0.27

Funding	7	38	0.57
Customers	9	39	0.58
Leaders	7	39	0.58
Extent	6	40	0.60
Poor	4	40	0.60
Size	4	40	0.60
Ability	7	43	0.64
Large	5	44	0.66
Planning	8	45	0.67
Owners	6	47	0.70
Employees	9	49	0.73
Explain	7	50	0.75
Perceive	8	51	0.76
Location	8	55	0.82
Owner	5	55	0.82
People	6	58	0.86
Lack	4	66	0.98
Contributing	12	67	1.00
Prevent	7	67	1.00
Perception	10	70	1.04
Leadership	10	100	1.49
Business	8	335	5.00
Failure	7	398	5.93
Businesses	10	435	6.49
Small	5	540	8.05

Appendix F
Reduction and Elimination of Interview Questions 10 to 15

IQ10: What is your perception and explanation about non-leadership factors, such as small business location, size, planning, and funding contributing to failure of small businesses?

IQ11: How do you perceive and explain small business location contributing to failure of small businesses?

IQ12: How do you perceive and explain the size of small businesses contributing to failure of small businesses?

IQ13: How do you perceive and explain culture of small businesses contributing to failure of small businesses?

IQ14: What is your perception and explanation of small business owner's difficulty in acquiring funding affects the ability to prevent failure of small businesses?

IQ15: To what extent do you believe poor planning by owner leader of a small business affects the ability to prevent failure of small businesses?

Themes	Participants
Non-Leadership factors cause failure of small businesses	1, 3, 5, 6, 10
Location	
Poor location includes poor strategic position, inaccessible and low populated areas cause failure of small businesses	1, 5, 6, 7, 9, 10
Size	
Overextended small business is hard to finance causing failure	1, 9
Culture	
Over-trusting employees cause failure of small businesses	1, 6
Family operated with least or no experience cause failure of small businesses	3, 6
Lack of versatility and creativity, such as same mindset can cause failure of small businesses	4, 6
Low culture-based consumption cause failure of small businesses	5, 6, 9
Difficulty in Acquiring Funds	
Bad credit, lack of collateral securities and loans result in failure of small businesses	3, 4, 6, 10
Lack of capital cause failure of small businesses	5, 6, 9
Lack of Planning	
Lack of knowledge and understanding	1, 6
Lack of business assessment for status	3, 9

Evans Nyatigo Ongaga

DM, MBA, BED (Arts)

Dr. Evans Nyatigo Ongaga, a holder of Doctor of Management in Organizational Leadership is currently working with New Haven Unified School District. Born to a minor family on 6th March 1970 in Nyamira County Kenya with 10 siblings, his parents were not rich but struggled to get-by. Evans' father, Stanley Ongaga Orina popularly known as Mokunyo was an elementary-middle school teacher while his mother practiced peasantry.

Evans started his Nursery school at Ramba Primary, Nyamira County Kenya in 1976. He Subsequently attended Standards 1 - 7 in Ramba Primary School and Forms 1 - 6 in Nyansiongo High School. He received his Bachelor of Education (Arts) Degree in Economics and History from Moi University (Maseno College), Kenya in 1990, MBA (Management in Information Systems) from Armstrong University, Oakland California, and Doctor of Management in Organizational Leadership from University of Phoenix Arizona.

Evans worked at St. Mathias Mulumba High school as a Business Education graduate teacher after Bachelors Degree (1994 - 1998). In 2001, Evans joined and worked with the Silicon Valley high tech companies, including Applied Materials, Coherent Laser Group, The Home Depot and Silicon valley Engineering Group, where he held positions of expedites, import and export processing, project and logistic manager respectively. Also, from 2010, he worked with San Jose Unified School District and Aspire Public Schools. Evans successfully defended and published his research dissertation " Failure of Small Businesses in San Jose, California: A Qualitative Phenomenological Study" before Chair and Committee Members in 2016.

 School of Advanced Studies
University of Phoenix

 American Journal *of*
Transformational Leadership

9 781722 000707